# Fundamentals of
# Data
# Normalization

→ ⟶» ↔ ⟶ → ⟶» ↔ ⟶ ⟶» ↔ ⟶

## Alan F. Dutka
## Howard H. Hanson

## ADDISON-WESLEY PUBLISHING COMPANY

Reading, Massachusetts • Menlo Park, California • New York
Don Mills, Ontario • Wokingham, England • Amsterdam • Bonn
Sydney • Singapore • Tokyo • Madrid • San Juan

**Library of Congress Cataloging-in-Publication Data**

Dutka, Alan F.
  Fundamentals of data normalization / by Alan F. Dutka,
  Howard H. Hanson.
      p.      cm.
  Bibliography: p.
  Includes index.
  ISBN 0-201-06645-9 :
  1. Data structures (Computer science) 2. Data base management.
I. Hanson, Howard H.  II. Title.
QA76.9.D35D88 1989
005.7'3—dc 19                                                    88–6244
                                                                    CIP

Reprinted with corrections August, 1989

BCDEFGHIJ–BA–89

# Preface

References to data normalization appear regularly in textbooks, professional journals, trade journals, and magazines of the computer industry. The majority of these references are either very theoretical or very superficial. Consequently, students and practitioners of database design have had little opportunity to master the objectives, techniques, and benefits of data normalization.

This book is intended to fill the gap between the theoretical and the superficial coverage of data normalization, providing a comprehensive introduction to data normalization. The intended audience includes students of database design, professionals responsible for designing and maintaining databases, end users involved in computer-related activities, and managers who wish to appreciate data normalization.

*Fundamentals of Data Normalization* can be used in the academic environment as the primary text for a "special topics" class in data normalization or as a supplementary text in a class in database design. It is also appropriate for independent study by technicians and managers in business, industry, and government.

The text is divided into three major parts: The Basics (Chapters 1 through 5), Implementing the Basics (Chapters 6 through 8), and Advanced Theory (Chapters 9 and 10 and the Appendix). The first five chapters provide the basic material required to understand and appreciate data normalization. A small but realistic application of data normalization is discussed in Chapter 6. A more comprehensive application is presented in Chapter 7. Implementation guidelines for traditional hierarchical and network environments are discussed in Chapter 8.

The Advanced Theory section, which is more technical, is geared to individuals with a mathematical background. This part is self-contained, allowing mathematical theory and notation to be kept to a minimum in the first eight chapters.

The book contains more than 300 exercises devoted exclusively to issues relevant to data normalization. The text and problems provide the material necessary to understand and implement data normalization in a realistic database environment.

## Acknowledgments

We wish to acknowledge the "real world" view of data normalization provided by Jim Mohney, John Bowen, and Dennis Riley of the Uniroyal-Goodrich Tire Company. Excellent critical comments were provided by Marilyn Bohl (Digital Research), Paul Winsberg (Codd & Date Consulting Group), and Kathi Hogshead Davis (Northern Illinois University). Diane Dutka (age 8) developed the data used in the Human Resources database in Chapter 7. Addison-Wesley's staff exhibited high standards of professionalism toward every aspect related to the publication of this book. The efforts of Stephanie Kaylin, the copy editor, were especially appreciated.

*Akron, Ohio*                                                      A. F. D.
                                                                   H. H. H.

# Contents

# Part I

# The Basics

The five chapters in this part provide the basic material required to understand and appreciate data normalization. The objective is to design stable databases that can accurately answer both planned and ad hoc inquiries and that are free of update problems.

This can be accomplished by understanding the structure of a relation and three types of data dependencies: functional, transitive and multivalued. The basic normal forms—first, second, third, Boyce-Codd and fourth—provide the structure to develop the desired database. Additional material regarding the join of two relations and the "lossless join" property is also required to ensure that the database serves its intended purpose.

# Chapter 1

# An Introduction to Data Normalization

Data normalization is a set of rules and techniques concerned with

- Identifying relationships among attributes,
- Combining attributes to form relations, and
- Combining relations to form a database.

An **attribute** (also called a **field**) is a data element. A **relation** is a group of attributes.

For example, a relation called PERSON may contain the attributes NAME, ADDRESS, DATE OF BIRTH, HEIGHT, WEIGHT, SALARY, etc. A Human Resources database may contain many relations such as PERSON, DEPENDENTS and DEPARTMENTS.

## 1.1 MODIFICATION ANOMALIES

A major objective of data normalization is to avoid modification anomalies. For example, an insertion anomaly occurs when the insertion of a fact about one attribute requires an additional fact about a second attribute. A deletion anomaly occurs when facts are lost about two attributes with one deletion.

A few examples will help illustrate modification anomalies. Suppose that the following attributes in a Marketing database are grouped together in one relation:

CUSTOMER NAME
CUSTOMER NUMBER
CUSTOMER ADDRESS
PRODUCT NUMBER
PRODUCT DESCRIPTION
PRODUCT PRICE

In order to insert information regarding a new product, a fictitious "dummy" customer must be created. Information about an existing product will be lost if all customer information corresponding to that product is deleted.

Grouping together the three attributes EMPLOYEE IDENTIFICATION NUMBER, DEPARTMENT NAME and DEPARTMENT MANAGER provides a second example. If the department changes managers, then information for every employee in the department must be modified. This problem can be eliminated by forming two groupings of information:

| Group 1 | Group 2 |
| --- | --- |
| EMPLOYEE IDENTIFICATION NUMBER | DEPARTMENT NAME |
| DEPARTMENT NAME | DEPARTMENT MANAGER |

Decomposing a set of attributes into smaller groups is one of the techniques used to reduce or eliminate modification anomalies.

Suppose that the following attributes are grouped together:

FOOTBALL PLAYER'S UNION IDENTIFICATION NUMBER
NAME OF TEAM
TEAM COACH
TEAM OWNER

Numerous update problems exist with this grouping. For example, if a team obtains a new coach or new owner, then the information for every player belonging to the team must be changed. If all the union players resign from the union, then information concerning the coach and owner is lost. The coach and owner names must be repeated each time a new union player is added. These modification problems are eliminated by forming two groups:

| Group 1 | Group 2 |
| --- | --- |
| FOOTBALL PLAYER'S UNION IDENTIFICATION NUMBER NAME OF TEAM | NAME OF TEAM TEAM COACH TEAM OWNER |

A student new to database design may assume that modification anomalies are rare or unusual. An experienced database designer, however, should have no problem relating to fictitious dummy records that are created to support the insertion of new data. Storage devices contain volumes of data that could be deleted except for a few fields that may still contain required information.

## 1.2 LOGICAL AND PHYSICAL DATABASE DESIGN

Data normalization is an analytical technique useful during logical database design. The viewpoints and requirements of the user are considered during the logical database design process. The appropriate attributes, and relationships among these attributes, are identified and defined. The user's view of the data should not be inhibited by technical hardware and software limitations. Thus hardware and software characteristics are not considered during logical database design.

Eventually the logical database design is implemented physically. Physical implementation is the first stage at which the particular characteristics of the database management system are considered. For example, departures from an ideal logical design may be justified by improved system performance. Data normalization will provide a clear understanding of the relevant attributes and the relationships among these attributes. This knowledge will benefit the technicians who are implementing the physical database.

## 1.3 APPLICATION DATABASES AND SUBJECT DATABASES

Database methodology continues to increase in sophistication. Early data processing applications utilized a separate file for each application. The design was generally simple and easy to implement. Such a design, however, results in data redundancy and high maintenance costs. Initial database technology was often used to create a separate database for each application. This approach improved data organization and helped reduce data redundancy. Application databases were widely used in the 1970s.

Subject databases provide an additional degree of sophistication. These databases relate to organizational subjects (e.g., products, customers, personnel) rather than to conventional computer applications (e.g., order entry, payroll, billing). A subject database is data driven rather than application driven. This kind of database is independent of any specific application and is shared by multiple applications. A large initial investment in analysis (including data normalization) is required. Future maintenance and enhancement activity, however, is reduced substantially.

Consider the three application databases in Fig. 1.1: a Payroll database, an Employment History database and a Medical Claims database. Each database is comprised of data common to all the applications. The data must be stored and maintained by all the applications.

Data redundancy increases physical storage requirements and the likelihood of update errors. For example, a change of address must be entered in three different databases. Inconsistencies may result if the definition of an attribute changes within the various application databases. For example, a "home address" may differ from a "mailing address." Multiple application databases may also cause other incompatibilities (e.g., different computer languages or different formats).

The combination of subject databases and application programs is illustrated in Fig. 1.2. Each application program uses data that is stored and maintained in one database. Ad hoc inquires will use the same data. Thus consistency is maintained among various applications.

Successful design of subject databases and comprehensive information systems usually incorporates both strategic data planning (to identify the required databases) and logical database design (to specify the logical record structure of those databases). Data normalization should be included as an integral part of the logical design process.

## 1.4  DATABASE MODELS

Databases are often classified as hierarchical, network or relational. **Hierarchical** models are also called tree structures (see Fig. 1.3a). A typical corporate organization chart is an example of a hierarchical model. The president of the company is at the top of the structure. Several vice presidents may report to the president. Director-level executives may report to the vice presidents. This reporting structure may continue for several additional levels of management.

The terms **parent** and **child** are often used in describing a hierarchical model. The president is the parent of the vice presidents, and each vice president may be the parent of several directors. A vice president is also a child of the president, while a director is a child of a vice president.

An important characteristic of the hierarchical model is that a child is associated with only one parent. The relationship between parent and child is one-to-many: A hierarchical business organization implies that an employee must report to only one supervisor.

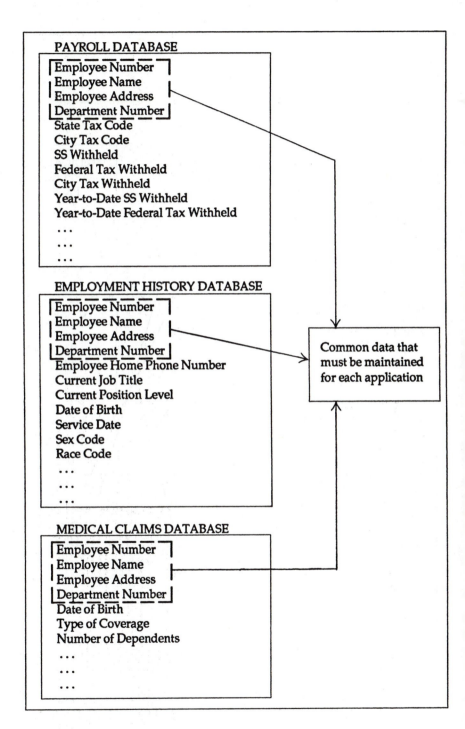

**Figure 1.1** Three applications databases.

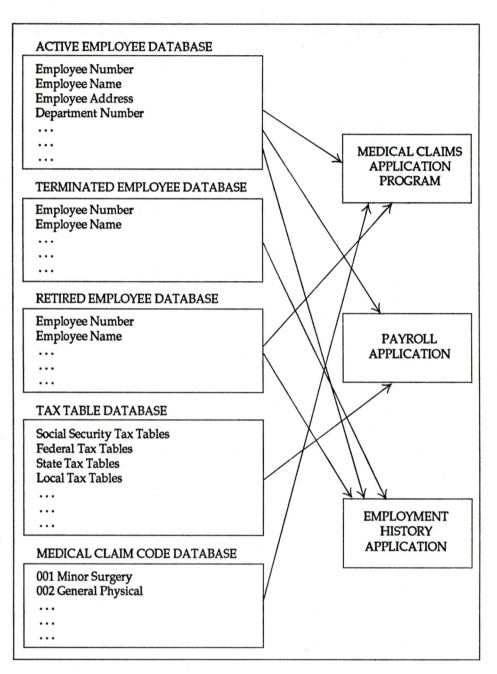

**Figure 1.2** Subject databases and applications programs.

A **network** model allows a child to be associated with more than one parent (see Fig. 1.3b). The relationship between students and classes in an example of a network structure. A student may enroll in more than one class, and most classes contain more than one student. A tree can be considered a special case of a network.

The distinction between hierarchical and network models is rapidly becoming obsolete. Software enhancements allow network models to be represented in the major hierarchical database systems. Consequently the database designer in a hierarchical environment has considerable flexibility.

The **relational** model is a significant departure from the hierarchical or network models. Relationships among attributes are represented in a tabular format using rows and columns (see Fig. 1.3c). The model is conceptually easier to understand than either the hierarchical or the network model. However, the hardware and software required to implement the relational model efficiently are limited.

Data normalization is a valuable logical design technique in hierarchical, network or relational database environments, although the normalization process is most often associated with relational databases. This has occurred since data normalization is defined in the context of the relational model. Also, during the initial implementation of hierarchical and network designs, the distinction between logical and physical design was not as prevalent. Techniques used in the logical design process (such as data normalization) were not emphasized in these earlier implementations. Data normalization will increase in importance as the relational structure gains acceptance and as the distinction between logical and physical design is incorporated in the database design process.

## 1.5 BENEFITS OF DATA NORMALIZATION

The major benefits of a correctly normalized database from the management informations systems (MIS) perspective include:

- Development of a strategy for constructing relations and selecting keys.
- Improved interfaces with end-user computing activities (e.g., ability to accommodate unplanned inquiries).
- Reduced problems associated with inserting and deleting data.
- Reduced enhancement and modification time associated with changing the data structure (e.g., adding or deleting attributes).

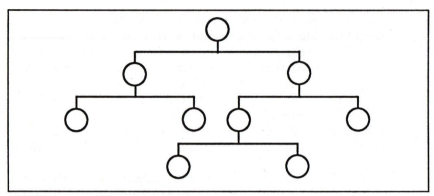

a. A Hierarchical Database Model

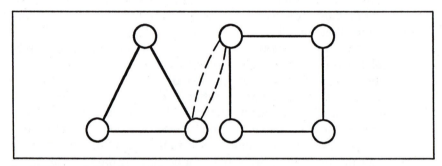

b. A Network Database Model

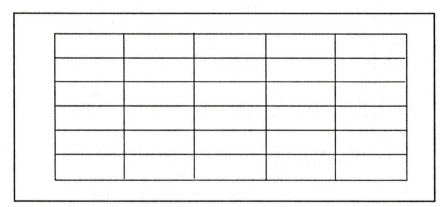

c. A Relational Database Model

**Figure 1.3** Database models.

- Improved information for decisions relating to physical database design.
- Identification of potential problems that may require additional analysis and documentation.

From the end user's perspective, a correctly normalized database will translate into improved response time from the MIS organization, as well as improved capabilities for end user computing activities.

A database contains facts and figures. Information is the knowledge derived from this data. Intelligent planning and decision making require accurate, reliable information. Data normalization is a major component used to transform data into information.

# Chapter 2

# The Structure of a Relation

The definitions and descriptions presented in this chapter are fundamental to understanding data normalization. Included are a discussion of the basic relational structure, a definition of functional dependence, a discussion of repeating groups and an introduction to relational operators. This material will be used throughout the text to define, describe and illustrate the data normalization process.

## 2.1 THE PROPERTIES OF A RELATION

A set of two-dimensional tables called **relations** is required in the normalization process. Relations are developed using the 14 structural properties presented in Fig. 2.1.

## 2.2 OTHER DEFINITIONS

The following definitions are also helpful in discussing data normalization:

The **union** of relations R and S is the set of all attributes contained in either R or S or in both. RS is used to denote the union of relations R and S.

The **intersection** of relations R and S is the set of all attributes contained in both R and S. R ∩ S is used to denote the intersection of relations R and S.

1. Columns (also called attributes) represent fields. Each column has a unique name.
2. Each column is homogeneous. Thus the entries in any column are all of the same type (e.g., age, name, employee number etc.).
3. Each column has a **domain**, the set of possible values that can appear in the column.
4. Rows (also called tuples) represent records. If a relation has $n$ columns, each row is an $n$-tuple.
5. The order of the rows and columns is not important.
6. No duplicate rows are allowed.
7. **Repeating groups** (collections of logically related attributes that occur multiple times within one record occurrence) are not allowed.
8. A **candidate key** is an attribute (or set of attributes) that uniquely identifies a row. A candidate key must possess the following properties:
   - **Unique identification:** For every row, the value of the key must uniquely identify that row.
   - **Nonredundancy:** No attribute in the key can be discarded without destroying the property of unique identification.
9. A **primary key** is a candidate key selected as the unique identifier. Every relation must contain a primary key. The primary key is usually the key selected to identify a row when the database is physically implemented. For example, a part number is selected instead of a part description.
10. A **superkey** is any set of attributes that uniquely identifies a row. A superkey differs from a candidate key in that the superkey does not require the nonredundancy property.
11. A **foreign key** is an attribute that appears as a nonkey attribute in one relation and as a primary key attribute (or part of a primary key) in another relation.
12. A **composite key** is a key that contains more than one attribute.
13. A **relational schema** is a set of attributes, dependencies and other constraints that characterizes a relation. Various types of dependencies and constraints are discussed throughout the book.
14. An **instance** of a relation is a set of rows that populate the relation. Updates to the database will change the instance of a relation over time. An instance is **valid** if all the dependencies and other constraints specified in the relational schema are satisfied.

**Figure 2.1** The structural properties of a relation.

The difference of relations R and S is the set of all attributes contained in relation R but not in relation S. R – S is used to denote the difference of relations R and S.

A decomposition of a relation R is a set of relations $R_i$ such that the union of relations $R_i$ is the relation R.

## 2.3 FUNCTIONAL DEPENDENCE

The following table represents the annual sales of a corporation over a 16-year period:

| YEAR | SALES (billions of dollars) | YEAR | SALES (billions of dollars) |
|------|------|------|------|
| 16 | 3.0 | 8 | 2.0 |
| 15 | 3.2 | 7 | 1.7 |
| 14 | 3.1 | 6 | 1.4 |
| 13 | 3.0 | 5 | 1.2 |
| 12 | 2.6 | 4 | 1.1 |
| 11 | 2.4 | 3 | 1.1 |
| 10 | 2.0 | 2 | 1.1 |
| 9 | 1.9 | 1 | 0.9 |

This data is in relational form. Each row contains two attributes (YEAR and SALES). The primary key attribute is YEAR. This relation (called SALESDATA) is represented using the following notation:

SALESDATA(YEAR, SALES)

In this format, the relation is named first. Each attribute is then identified; the primary key attribute(s) are underlined.

Only one sales value exists for a specific year. More than one year, however, may be associated with the same value of sales. For example, the sales value 3.0 is associated with both year 16 and year 13. Thus YEAR determines SALES but SALES does not determine YEAR. SALES is a function of YEAR (i.e., SALES depends upon YEAR). If SALES is represented as $y$ and YEAR as $x$, the familiar mathematical expression $y = f(x)$ represents the functional relationship between $y$ and $x$. Thus a discrete mathematical function may be displayed as a relation.

The 16 values in the SALES attribute are a subset of the domain SALES. Understanding the domain of an attribute is important both in determining the size of the corresponding field and in checking the validity of data. Knowledge of the domain is also used in advanced normalization theory.

Functional dependence in relational terminology can be defined formally as follows:

> For any relation R, attribute A is **functionally dependent** on attribute B if, for every valid instance, the value of B determines the value of A.

The phrase "for every valid instance" ensures that the functional dependency is valid irrespective of any insertions or deletions. The functional dependence of A on B is represented by an arrow as follows: $B \rightarrow A$. Thus YEAR $\rightarrow$ SALES. The notation $B \nrightarrow A$ is used to denote that A is not functionally dependent on B.

An instance does not imply a dependency. However, dependencies imply valid instances. An instance cannot be used to show that a dependency is true but can be used to demonstrate that a dependency is false.

An attribute can be functionally dependent on a group of attributes rather than on a single attribute.

> An attribute (or group of attributes) X is **fully functionally dependent** on another collection of attributes Y, if X is functionally dependent on the whole of Y but not on any subset of Y.

Functional dependence is not limited to numerical data. For example, consider the relation AIRPORT(NAME, CITY) with the following instance:

| NAME | CITY |
|------|------|
| LaGuardia | New York |
| Hopkins | Cleveland |
| J. F. Kennedy | New York |
| Logan | Boston |
| Burke Lakefront | Cleveland |
| L.A. International | Los Angeles |

Each airport name is unique, but more than one airport can be associated with a given city. Thus CITY is functionally dependent on NAME but NAME is not functionally dependent on CITY. These facts are expressed in the following ways:

$$\begin{array}{ll} \text{CITY} = f(\text{NAME}) & \text{NAME} \neq f(\text{CITY}) \\ \text{NAME} \to \text{CITY} & \text{CITY} \nrightarrow \text{NAME} \end{array}$$

## 2.4 INFERENCE AXIOMS FOR FUNCTIONAL DEPENDENCIES

A given set of functional dependencies will usually generate additional, implied functional dependencies. For example, $X \to Z$ can be inferred from the dependencies $X \to Y$ and $Y \to Z$. Sets of inference axioms associated with functional dependencies were developed by W. W. Armstrong ("Dependency Structures of Database Relationships," *Proceedings, IFIP Congress* 1974) and by C. Berri, R. Fagin and J. H. Howard ("A Complete Axiomatization for Functional and Multivalued Dependencies in Database Relations," *Proceedings, 1977 ACM SIGMOD International Conference on Management of Data*, Toronto, August 1977). These axioms are presented in Fig. 2.2. All possible functional dependencies implied by a given set can be generated using these axioms.

Suppose that A, B, C, D and E are attributes with the following dependencies:

$$\begin{array}{l} A \to B \\ CD \to A \\ C \to E \\ E \to C \\ BD \to C \end{array}$$

Some of the dependencies implied by the inference axioms are:

$$\begin{array}{ll} A & \to A \text{ (axiom 1)} \\ AC & \to B \text{ (axiom 2)} \\ CD & \to AE \text{ (axioms 2 and 3)} \\ AD & \to C \text{ (axiom 6)} \\ DE & \to A \text{ (axiom 6)} \\ CD & \to B \text{ (axiom 5)} \\ BD & \to E \text{ (axiom 5)} \\ ED & \to A \text{ (axiom 6)} \\ AD & \to E \text{ (axioms 5 and 6)} \\ DE & \to B \text{ (axioms 5 and 6)} \end{array}$$

Functional dependencies also exist that are trivially true. Trivial functional dependencies occur when a set of attributes implies a subset of the

> Let X, Y, Z and W represent subsets of the attributes that comprise the database. Then:
>
> 1. Reflexive rule           $X \to X$
> 2. Augmentation rule        if $X \to Y$, then $XZ \to Y$
> 3. Union rule               if $X \to Y$ and $X \to Z$, then $X \to YZ$
> 4. Decomposition rule       if $X \to Y$, then $X \to Z$ where Z is a subset of Y
> 5. Transitivity rule        if $X \to Y$ and $Y \to Z$, then $X \to Z$
> 6. Pseudotransitivity rule  if $X \to Y$ and $YZ \to W$, then $XZ \to W$

**Figure 2.2** Inference axioms for functional dependencies.

same set (e.g., $XY \to X$). A trivial dependency is always true for every instance. The dependency is trivial because duplicate rows in XY will also be duplicate rows in X and Y individually.

## 2.5 REPEATING GROUPS

A **repeating group** is a collection of logically related attributes that occur multiple times within one row.

Examples of repeating groups include names of employee dependents, products associated with an invoice and employee's career- interest designations. A repeating group is often characterized by an OCCURS clause in COBOL, an array in FORTRAN or a structure in C.

For example, consider the following attributes that relate to an employee benefit program:

| | |
|---|---|
| ESSNUM | employee number |
| ENAME | employee name |
| PCODE | code for benefit plan type |
| DNAME | dependent name |
| DBIRTHD | dependent birth date |
| DSEX | dependent sex |

The attributes DNAME, DBIRTHD and DSEX comprise a repeating group that is duplicated for each dependent. The repeating group can be represented in COBOL with an OCCURS clause:

```
01 EMPLOYEE DEPENDENTS RECORD
      03 ESSNUM
      03 ENAME
      03 PCODE
03 DEPENDENT DATA OCCURS 10 TIMES
      05 DNAME
      05 DBIRTHD
      05 DSEX
```

The repeating group can be represented in FORTRAN using an array. For example,

```
(ESSNUM(I), ENAME(I), PCODE(I), M(I), {DNAME(I,J),
DBIRTHD(I,J), DSEX(I,J), J=1,M(I)})
```

where M(I) represents the number of dependents associated with the Ith employee and DNAME(I,J) represents the name of the Jth dependent for the Ith employee.

The representation of the repeating group in C can be accomplished with the following structure:

```
struct employee
{
     int essnum;
     char ename[30];
     char pcode;
     struct dep_rec
     {
          char dname[30];
          char dbirthd[6];
          char dsex;
     } emp_deps[10];
};
```

A relational representation begins with a grouping of attributes as follows:

BENEFITS(ESSNUM, ENAME, PCODE, DNAME, DBIRTHD, DSEX)

The repeating group is eliminated by creating two relations:

BENEFITS(ESSNUM, ENAME, PCODE)
DEPENDENTS(ESSNUM, DNAME, DBIRTHD, DSEX)

An employee number, name and plan code are entered once for each employee. The dependent data is entered in separate relations. DNAME is used to identify a particular dependent. The ESSNUM attribute is used to connect the BENEFITS and DEPENDENTS relations.

## 2.6 RELATIONAL OPERATORS

Relational operators are used to manipulate relations in a manner similar to the way arithmetic operators (plus, minus, multiply and divide) are used to manipulate numbers. The relational operators projection and join are especially important in data normalization.

A relation can be decomposed into new relations that consist of subsets of the attributes in the original relation. This is accomplished by using the projection operator. Consider the following instance of the relation EMPLOYEE(NUM, NAME, DEPT, SALARY):

| NUM | NAME | DEPT | SALARY |
|-----|------|------|--------|
| 101 | Charles Miller | Accounting | 35,000 |
| 102 | Fawaz Ghumrawi | Accounting | 40,000 |
| 103 | Shelly Knight | Marketing | 40,000 |
| 104 | Michael Rodriquez | Human Relations | 38,000 |
| 105 | Clair Schler | Accounting | 40,000 |

The projection of this instance onto the attributes DEPT and SALARY will result in the following instance of a new relation:

| DEPT | SALARY |
|------|--------|
| Accounting | 35,000 |
| Accounting | 40,000 |
| Marketing | 40,000 |
| Human Relations | 38,000 |

The new relation contains the two attributes specified (DEPT and SALARY). Note that the number of rows is reduced since the duplicate row (Accounting, 40,000) was eliminated from the new instance. This projection answers the question "How many unique DEPT and SALARY combinations exist?" but is inappropriate for responding to commands such as "List all the salaries for employees in the Marketing Department."

The projection operator is concerned with the attributes in a relation. A similar operator, selection, is concerned with the rows in a relation. The selection operator, used extensively in database queries, is discussed in Chapter 7. A third operator, join, is used to combine data from two relations. The join operator is discussed extensively beginning in Chapter 5.

## Summary

A set of definitions and descriptions is necessary to understand the normalization process. A relation is represented as a table containing rows and columns of data. The rows and columns of a valid relational structure must possess specific properties. Definitions of a candidate key, primary key, superkey, foreign key and composite key are also required. The dependency structure among the attributes must be defined clearly. Functional dependence is the initial criterion used to define the dependency structure among attributes.

## Exercises

**2.1** Do the following tables represent relations? Explain each answer.

a.

| COMPANY | NUMBER | NAME | TYPE |
|---|---|---|---|
| Midwest Life | 1-234-6 | Smith | Full |
| | 1-893-2 | Jones | Liability |
| Southeast Life | 10-35-99 | Black | Limited |

b.

| A | B | C | D |
|---|---|---|---|
| 1 | 10 | 3 | 2 |
| 5 | 6 | 8 | 9 |
| 3 | 7 | 20 | 15 |
| 35 | 22 | 7 | 18 |
| 5 | 6 | 8 | 9 |
| 4 | 2 | 1 | 15 |

c.

| A | B | C |
|---|---|---|
| 16,320 | 44.3 | 22% |
| 44,781 | 19.8 | 16.5 |
| 22% | 38.1 | 19,805 |

**2.2** Consider relation EMPLOYEE(NUM, NAME, SALARY). Is the employee number (NUM) functionally dependent on either NAME or SALARY or on both? Explain your answer.

**2.3** Consider relation STUDENT(NUM, NAME, ADVISOR). Assuming that a student may have only one advisor:

  a. Is ADVISOR functionally dependent on NUM?

  b. Is NUM functionally dependent on ADVISOR?

**2.4** Consider relation CLASS(STUDENTNUM, CLASSNAME, GRADE). What is the functional dependence between GRADE and the attributes in the primary key?

**2.5** Consider relation STUDENT(NUM, NAME, ADVISOR).

  a. Which candidate keys will identify a student?

  b. Can the combination NAME and NUM be used as a candidate key? Explain your answer.

**2.6** Consider the following instance of relation R(A, B, C):

| A | B | C |
|---|---|---|
| 2 | 4 | 1 |
| 4 | 4 | 3 |
| 6 | 4 | 3 |
| 8 | 3 | 7 |
| 10 | 1 | 9 |

Determine which of the following dependencies do not hold:

$$A \rightarrow B, A \rightarrow C, B \rightarrow A, B \rightarrow C, C \rightarrow A \text{ and } C \rightarrow B$$

**2.7** Find the functional dependencies that are not violated (if any exist) in the following instance of relation R(A, B, C):

| A | B | C |
|---|---|---|
| 1 | 2 | 3 |
| 1 | 3 | 4 |
| 2 | 3 | 5 |
| 4 | 5 | 5 |
| 6 | 5 | 5 |

**2.8** Given relational schema R(A, B, C), A → B, determine which of the following dependencies are implied by the inference axioms. State the appropriate axioms if the dependency is implied.

    a. $AC \rightarrow B$

    b. $B \rightarrow C$

    c. $B \rightarrow B$

    d. $A \rightarrow BC$

    e. $B \rightarrow A$

**2.9** Given relational schema R(A, B, C, D), $A \rightarrow B$ and $A \rightarrow C$, determine which of the following dependencies are implied by the inference axioms. State the appropriate axioms if the dependency is implied.

    a. $A \rightarrow BC$

    b. $A \rightarrow BCD$

    c. $AD \rightarrow B$

    d. $BC \rightarrow A$

    e. $AB \rightarrow B$

**2.10** Given relational schema R(A, B, C, D), $A \rightarrow BC$, determine which of the following dependencies are implied by the inference axioms. State the appropriate axioms if the dependency is implied.

    a. $A \rightarrow B$

    b. $AD \rightarrow BC$

    c. $B \rightarrow C$

    d. $AC \rightarrow B$

    e. $A \rightarrow D$

**2.11** Given relational schema R(A, B, C, D), $A \rightarrow B$ and $B \rightarrow C$, determine which of the following dependencies are implied by the inference axioms. State the appropriate axioms if the dependency is implied.

    a. $A \rightarrow C$

    b. $A \rightarrow BC$

    c. $ACD \rightarrow B$

    d. $AC \rightarrow B$

    e. $AD \rightarrow BC$

**2.12** Given relational schema R(A, B, C, D), $A \rightarrow B$ and $BC \rightarrow D$, determine which of the following dependencies are implied by the inference axioms. State the appropriate axioms if the dependency is implied.

    a. $AC \rightarrow D$

    b. $A \rightarrow D$

    c. $C \rightarrow D$

    d. $AD \rightarrow B$

    e. $AD \rightarrow C$

**2.13** Consider the following attributes:

| | |
|---|---|
| INUM | invoice number |
| IDATE | invoice date |
| CNUM | customer number |
| ITEMN | item number |
| QUANT | item quantity |
| PRICE | item price |

A COBOL representation of these attributes follows:

```
01 INVOICE INFORMATION
   03 INUM
   03 IDATE
   03 CNUM
   03 LINE ITEM DATA OCCURS 20 TIMES
      05 ITEMN
      05 QUANT
      05 PRICE
```

A FORTRAN representation follows:

```
(INUM(I), IDATE(I), CNUM(I), M(I), {ITEMN(I,J),
QUANT(I,J), PRICE(I,J), J=1,M(I)})
```

A C representation follows:

```
struct invoice
{
    char inum[10];
    char idate[6];
    char cnum[6];
    struct item_data
    {
        char itemn[10];
        int quant;
        int price;
    } line_item[20];
};
```

Develop a relational representation for this data.

**2.14** Given attributes A, B, C, D, give an instance of at least two rows that satisfies:

a. $A \rightarrow B$ and $C \rightarrow D$

b. $A \rightarrow B$ and $C \nrightarrow D$

   c. A $\twoheadrightarrow$ B and C $\rightarrow$ D

   d. A $\twoheadrightarrow$ B and C $\twoheadrightarrow$ D

**2.15** Consider the following instance of relation R(A, B, C):

| A | B | C |
|---|---|---|
| 1 | 1 | 1 |
| 1 | 2 | 2 |
| 1 | 3 | 3 |
| 1 | 1 | 2 |
| 1 | 2 | 1 |

   a. What is the projection of R on R1 = A?

   b. What is the projection of R on R2 = B?

   c. What is the projection of R on R3 = C?

   d. What is the projection of R on R4 = AB?

   e. What is the projection of R on R5 = AC?

**2.16** Determine which of the following examples are valid instances of relational schema R(A, B, C, D), A $\rightarrow$ B and BC $\rightarrow$ D. If an instance is not valid, explain why this is the case.

a.

| A | B | C | D |
|---|---|---|---|
| 1 | 1 | 1 | 1 |
| 1 | 1 | 1 | 2 |
| 2 | 2 | 2 | 2 |
| 2 | 2 | 2 | 3 |

b.

| A | B | C | D |
|---|---|---|---|
| 1 | 1 | 1 | 1 |
| 1 | 1 | 1 | 2 |
| 1 | 2 | 1 | 2 |
| 2 | 2 | 1 | 1 |

c.

| A | B | C | D |
|---|---|---|---|
| 1 | 1 | 1 | 1 |
| 1 | 1 | 1 | 2 |
| 2 | 2 | 1 | 1 |
| 2 | 2 | 1 | 2 |
| 3 | 2 | 1 | 2 |

d.

| A | B | C | D |
|---|---|---|---|
| 1 | 1 | 1 | 2 |
| 2 | 1 | 1 | 2 |
| 3 | 2 | 1 | 1 |
| 3 | 2 | 2 | 2 |

**2.17** Find the union, intersection and differences of the following pairs of relations:

   a. R1(A, B, C, D)        R2(A, E, F, G)

   b. R1(A, B, C, D)        R2(A, B, C, D)

   c. R1(A, B, C, D)        R2(A, B)

   d. R1(A, B, C)          R2(D, E, F)

   e. R1(A, C, D)          R2(A, B, C)

# Chapter 3

# First, Second and Third Normal Forms

A major objective of data normalization is to eliminate update anomalies. The first three normal forms progress in a systematic manner toward achieving this objective. More subtle types of anomalies, however, continue to be discovered. Thus the first three normal forms provide an excellent way to begin to learn the normalization process. Advanced normal forms that address more subtle anomalies are introduced in later chapters.

## 3.1 FIRST NORMAL FORM

A relation is in **first normal form** if it contains no repeating groups.

Relations only in first normal form suffer serious problems associated with insertions and deletions. For example, the following relation might be used by a university in developing a student and class database:

SCL(<u>SNUM, CNUM</u>, SNAME, SMAJ, TIME, BLDG)

where

SNUM = student number
CNUM = class number
SNAME = student name
SMAJ = student major
TIME = class time
BLDG = class building location

All the data concerning a student will be deleted if the student withdraws from all of his or her classes. Thus data regarding student number, name and major will be lost. Insertions are also a problem. Data regarding class time and building location cannot be entered until a student enrolls in the class.

A problem with the SCL relation is that nonkey attributes are dependent on various parts of the primary key but not on the entire key. For example,

$$SNUM \rightarrow SNAME \text{ but } CNUM \nrightarrow SNAME$$
$$SNUM \rightarrow SMAJ \text{ but } CNUM \nrightarrow SMAJ$$
$$CNUM \rightarrow TIME \text{ but } SNUM \nrightarrow TIME$$
$$CNUM \rightarrow BLDG \text{ but } SNUM \nrightarrow BLDG$$

The normalization process must continue beyond first normal form in order to eliminate undesirable insertion and deletion problems.

## 3.2 SECOND NORMAL FORM

A relation is in **second normal form** if the relation is in first normal form and every nonkey attribute is fully functionally dependent upon the primary key. Thus no nonkey attribute can be functionally dependent on part of the primary key.

A relation in first normal form will be in second normal form if any one of the following applies:

1. The primary key is composed of only one attribute.
2. No nonkey attributes exist.
3. Every nonkey attribute is dependent on the entire set of primary key attributes.

The SCL relation can be decomposed into three new relations as follows:

$$SINFO \text{ (\underline{SNUM}, SNAME, SMAJ)}$$
$$CINFO \text{ (\underline{CNUM}, TIME, BLDG)}$$
$$STUCLASS \text{ (\underline{SNUM, CNUM})}$$

The primary keys for both the SINFO and CINFO relations consist of just one attribute. The STUCLASS relation contains no nonkey attributes. Thus the relations are in second normal form.

Student data can be entered into the SINFO relation before the student enrolls in a class. Class data can be entered into the CINFO relation before any student enrolls in the class. Deletion of all students in a particular class in the STUCLASS relation will not result in either class or student data being deleted. Deletion of all classes for a particular student will not result in the loss of student data.

Elimination of the insertion and deletion problems is not entirely due to second normal form. Actually the relations are also in third normal form. The differences between second and third normal form can be illustrated by considering another potential relation in the student and class database:

MAJOR(SNUM, MAJDEPT, COLLEGE)

The primary key consists of a single attribute, and thus this relation must be in second normal form. A typical instance is:

| SNUM | MAJDEPT | COLLEGE |
|-------|------------|--------------|
| 91001 | Statistics | Science |
| 81062 | English | Liberal Arts |
| 83719 | Music | Liberal Arts |
| 94201 | Statistics | Science |
| 86319 | Music | Liberal Arts |
| 97001 | Statistics | Science |

Note the following:

- If student 81062 is deleted, the fact that the English Department is in the Liberal Arts College is lost.
- Several rows must be changed if the Statistics Department moves to the Engineering College.
- The fact that the Electrical Engineering Department is in the Engineering College cannot be entered until a student with that major is added.

These problems appear similar to those encountered with relations only in first normal form. Actually the problems are caused by a different type of dependency. The difficulty is that a dependency exists (MAJDEPT → COLLEGE) that does not involve the primary key. This dependency allows the attribute SNUM to determine COLLEGE in two ways:

1. SNUM → COLLEGE
2. SNUM → MAJDEPT → COLLEGE

The second structure creates the insertion and deletion problems. For example, if a student drops all classes, the deletion of SNUM could result in a loss of data regarding the MAJDEPT and COLLEGE relationship. Thus the normalization process must continue in order to eliminate these undesirable dependencies.

## 3.3 THIRD NORMAL FORM

A relation is in **third normal form** if, for every nontrivial functional dependency $X \rightarrow A$, either:

- The set of attributes, x, is a superkey, or
- Attribute A is a member of a candidate key.

Third normal form is often described as a situation in which an attribute is "a function of the key, the whole key and nothing but the key." This description captures the essence of third normal form but is difficult to define precisely and is also partially incorrect.

An attribute is a "function of the key, the whole key and nothing but the key" if the following two conditions are true:

1. Every nonkey attribute depends on the entire primary key.
2. No nonkey attribute is functionally dependent on another nonkey attribute.

These conditions, however, are too restrictive. A relation can be in third normal form even if a dependency exists among nonkey attributes. This occurs if all possible values of the implying attribute are unique (e.g., the implying attribute is a candidate key). For example, the relation

R(<u>SSNUM</u>, NAME, DEPTNUM)

is in third normal form if NAME $\rightarrow$ DEPTNUM and NAME is guaranteed never to contain duplicate values.

The second condition also becomes somewhat complicated if sets of attributes are considered. The condition should actually be stated as, "no nonkey attribute is functionally dependent on a set of attributes that does not contain a key."

Third normal form is often described by introducing a concept called transitive dependencies.

Consider the relation R ($\underline{A}$, B, C). Attribute C is **transitively dependent** on attribute A if attribute B satisfies:

$$A \rightarrow B$$
$$B \rightarrow C$$
$$B \not\rightarrow A$$

A relation in second normal form is in third normal form if no transitive dependencies exist.

The dependency $B \rightarrow C$ represents the potential problem in the relation (i.e., functional dependence among nonkey attributes). Attribute B is not a candidate key since $B \not\rightarrow A$, and thus the relation is not in third normal form.

Eliminating transitive dependencies will eliminate anomalies of the following nature: If $A \rightarrow B \rightarrow C$, then a B value cannot be associated with an A value unless a C value is also associated with a B value. Thus an $A \rightarrow B$ association cannot be inserted unless a $B \rightarrow C$ association is also inserted. Conversely, if a C value associated with a B value is deleted, then the corresponding $A \rightarrow B$ association may be lost.

The relation MAJOR(SNUM, MAJDEPT, COLLEGE), discussed in the previous section, can be decomposed into two new relations that are both in third normal form:

SMAJ(SNUM, MAJDEPT)
MDEPT(MAJDEPT, COLLEGE)

Transitive dependencies may also occur between sets of attributes. For example, consider the relation

SHIPMENT(NUM, ORIGIN, DESTINATION, DISTANCE)

which might be used by a transportation company to record shipment order numbers and origin, destination and distance data. An instance of this relation is:

| NUM | ORIGIN | DESTINATION | DISTANCE |
|-----|--------|-------------|----------|
| 101 | Atlanta | Boston | 1,088 |
| 102 | Atlanta | Boston | 1,088 |
| 103 | St. Louis | Chicago | 288 |
| 104 | Cleveland | Dallas | 1,187 |
| 105 | Los Angeles | San Francisco | 403 |
| 106 | Kansas City | Memphis | 459 |

Note that ORIGIN, DESTINATION and DISTANCE are not functionally dependent on each other when the attributes are considered in a pairwise manner. However, the combination of ORIGIN and DESTINATION determines DISTANCE. Since this dependency exists, the rows that contain duplicates of the ORIGIN, DESTINATION combination also contain duplicates of DISTANCE.

The SHIPMENT relation can be decomposed into two relations (each in third normal form) as follows:

SHIPMENT(<u>NUM</u>, ORIGIN, DESTINATION)
DISTANCE(<u>ORIGIN</u>, <u>DESTINATION</u>, DISTANCE)

The fact that the distance between New Orleans and Pittsburgh is 1,093 miles can then be added to the database even though a corresponding shipment order does not exist. This flexibility is desirable when analyzing "what-if" questions. Shipments can also be deleted without loss of the distance data. The distance between reoccurring origin and destination combinations need not be entered with each shipment.

## 3.4 EXAMPLES

Three examples are presented in this section to illustrate how relations in third normal form are constructed. The chapter concludes with some general guidelines for developing relations in third normal form.

**Example 3.1:** Credit History for Consumer Loans

This example involves enhancing an existing database used to record consumer loan history by individual. The current database allows space for a maximum of three loans per individual. A major objective is to expand the historical capabilities so that a complete loan record is available for each individual. The attributes associated with this example are illustrated in Fig. 3.1.

A repeating group associated with amount, date and payment rating must be eliminated. The attributes DL1, DL2 and DL3 can be replaced by the attribute DATE. Similarly, RL1, RL2 and RL3 can be replaced by PAYMENT RATING, and AMTL1, AMTL2 and AMTL3 can be replaced by AMOUNT.

The functional dependencies are:

$$SSNUM, DATE \rightarrow AMOUNT$$
$$SSNUM, DATE \rightarrow PAYMENT\ RATING$$
$$SSNUM \rightarrow NAME$$
$$SSNUM \rightarrow ADDRESS$$
$$SSNUM \rightarrow CITY$$
$$SSNUM \rightarrow ZIP$$
$$ZIP \rightarrow STATE$$

Three relations, each in third normal form, can be developed:

R1(<u>SSNUM, DATE,</u> AMOUNT, PAYMENT RATING)
R2(<u>SSNUM,</u> NAME, ADDRESS, CITY, ZIP)
R3(<u>ZIP,</u> STATE)

The loan information is no longer restricted to a maximum of three loans per individual. However, relation R1 assumes that at most one loan per day can be granted to any one individual.

| | |
|---|---|
| NAME | Name of person |
| SSNUM | Social security number of person |
| ADDRESS | Address where person resides |
| CITY | City where person resides |
| STATE | State where person resides |
| ZIP | Zip code where person resides |
| | |
| AMTL1 | Amount of most recent loan |
| DL1 | Date of most recent loan |
| RL1 | Payment rating for most recent loan |
| | |
| AMTL2 | Amount of second most recent loan |
| DL2 | Date of second most recent loan |
| RL2 | Payment rating for second most recent loan |
| | |
| AMTL3 | Amount of third most recent loan |
| DL3 | Date of third most recent loan |
| RL3 | Payment rating for third most recent loan |

**Figure 3.1** Attributes associated with Example 3.1.

**Example 3.2:** Manufacturing Specifications

This example involves the machines, setup times, production times and name and amount of each ingredient used in manufacturing a specific product. The number of machines and ingredients varies depending on the individual product. At most three machines and two ingredients, however, are used in any one product. The attributes identified by a systems analyst are presented in Fig. 3.2.

Two repeating groups must be eliminated:

1. Number, setup time and production time for each machine.
2. Number and amount of each ingredient.

The attribute names should be simplified as follows:

1. Replace MACNUM1, MACNUM2 and MACNUM3 with MACNUM.
2. Replace SETUP1, SETUP2 and SETUP3 with SETUP.
3. Replace PRORATE1, PRORATE2 and PRORATE3 with PRORATE.
4. Replace IGD1 and IGD2 with IGD.
5. Replace AMT1 and AMT2 with AMT.

The functional dependencies are:

$$
\begin{aligned}
\text{NUM, MACNUM} &\rightarrow \text{SETUP} \\
\text{NUM, MACNUM} &\rightarrow \text{PRORATE} \\
\text{NUM} &\rightarrow \text{DES} \\
\text{NUM, IGD} &\rightarrow \text{AMT}
\end{aligned}
$$

The following relations are each in third normal form:

R1(<u>NUM, MACNUM</u>, SETUP, PRORATE)
R2(<u>NUM, IGD</u>, AMT)
R3(<u>NUM</u>, DES)

Note that setup time is dependent on both machine and product but not upon the previously produced product on a particular machine.

The database also does not capture any information relating to the order in which the machines or ingredients are used.

| | |
|---|---|
| NUM | Product number |
| DES | Product description |
| | |
| MACNUM1 | Number of first machine used |
| SETUP1 | Setup time for first machine |
| PRORATE1 | Production time for first machine |
| | |
| MACNUM2 | Number of second machine used |
| SETUP2 | Setup time for second machine |
| PRORATE2 | Production time for second machine |
| | |
| MACNUM3 | Number of third machine used |
| SETUP3 | Setup time for third machine |
| PRORATE3 | Production time for third machine |
| | |
| IGD1 | Number of first ingredient used |
| AMT1 | Amount of first ingredient used |
| | |
| IGD2 | Number of second ingredient used |
| AMT2 | Amount of second ingredient used |

**Figure 3.2** Attributes associated with Example 3.2.

**Example 3.3:** An Inventory of Personal Computer Hardware and Software

This example involves a database to store information concerning personal computer hardware and software used by employees. An expert "contact" person for each software product is included, along with the expert's rating of the software. The attributes associated with this example are presented in Fig. 3.3.

The functional dependencies are:

$$
\begin{aligned}
\text{UFN, ULN} &\rightarrow \text{ULOC} \\
\text{UFN, ULN} &\rightarrow \text{UDIV} \\
\text{UFN, ULN} &\rightarrow \text{UEXT} \\
\text{CPER} &\rightarrow \text{CEXT} \\
\text{CPER} &\rightarrow \text{CLOC} \\
\text{SNAME} &\rightarrow \text{STYPE} \\
\text{CPER, SNAME, SVER} &\rightarrow \text{SRATE} \\
\text{UFN, ULN, HPUR, SNAME, SVER} &\rightarrow \text{SPUR} \\
\text{SNAME, SVER} &\rightarrow \text{CPER}
\end{aligned}
$$

| | |
|---|---|
| UFN | User's first name |
| ULN | User's last name |
| UDIV | User's work division number |
| UEXT | User's telephone extension |
| ULOC | User's work location |
| | |
| CPER | Contact person (individual knowledgeable about the software) |
| CEXT | Contact person's telephone extension |
| CLOC | Contact person's work location |
| | |
| HPUR | Date hardware was purchased |
| HTYPE | Type of hardware (e.g., XT, AT, PS/2) |
| | |
| SNAME | Name of software (e.g., Lotus 1-2-3) |
| SPUR | Date software was purchased |
| SRATE | Software rating (opinion of contact person) |
| STYPE | Type of software (e.g., spreadsheet, database) |
| SVER | Version number of software |

**Figure 3.3** Attributes associated with Example 3.3.

Note that HTYPE was not included in the functional dependencies and thus must be included in a relation containing all key attributes.

Two repeating groups must be eliminated:

1. Hardware type and date of purchase.
2. Software information (SNAME, SPUR, SRATE, STYPE and SVER).

Elimination of the repeating groups is accomplished with the following two relations:

R1(UFN, ULN, HTYPE, HPUR)
R2(UFN, ULN, HPUR, SNAME, SVER, STYPE, SPUR, SRATE, CPER, CEXT, CLOC)

Relation R1 assumes that an employee purchases no more than one given hardware type on a given day. If HPUR was not included in the primary key, the assumption would be that an individual will purchase at most one given hardware type. R1 also assumes that an individual is uniquely identified by first and last name.

Relation R2 assumes that only one version of a particular software product is installed on any one machine. This relation must be further decomposed since CPER → CEXT and CPER → CLOC. Thus R2 is decomposed into

> R3(<u>UFN, ULN, HPUR, SNAME, SVER,</u> STYPE, SPUR, SRATE, CPER)
> R4(<u>CPER,</u> CEXT, CLOC)

Note in relation R3 that STYPE is a function of SNAME but not of UFN, ULN, HPUR and SVER. Thus R3 is further decomposed as follows:

> R5(<u>UFN, ULN, HPUR, SNAME, SVER,</u> SPUR, SRATE, CPER)
> R6(<u>SNAME,</u> STYPE)

Since the contact person provides the software rating, R5 is further decomposed:

> R7(<u>UFN, ULN, HPUR, SNAME, SVER,</u> SPUR, CPER)
> R8(<u>CPER, SNAME, SVER,</u> SRATE)

The contact person provides a software rating independently of any hardware. Thus R7 is further decomposed:

> R9(<u>UFN, ULN, HPUR, SNAME, SVER,</u> SPUR)
> R10(<u>SNAME, SVER,</u> CPER)

Information about the user can be incorporated in the following relation:

> R11(<u>UFN, ULN,</u> ULOC, UDIV, UEXT)

The database now contains seven relations:

> R1(<u>UFN, ULN, HTYPE, HPUR</u>)
> R4(<u>CPER,</u> CEXT, CLOC)
> R6(<u>SNAME,</u> STYPE)
> R8(<u>CPER, SNAME, SVER,</u> SRATE)
> R9(<u>UFN, ULN, HPUR, SNAME, SVER,</u> SPUR)
> R10(<u>SNAME, SVER,</u> CPER)
> R11(<u>UFN, ULN,</u> ULOC, UDIV, UEXT)

Another modification to the database is required. The attribute CPER is not necessary in the key of relation R8. SNAME and SVER are the only attributes needed since SNAME, SVER → CPER. The original dependency CPER, SNAME, SVER → SRATE should be replaced by SNAME, SVER → SRATE since the inclusion of CPER creates a trivial dependency. Relations R8 and R10 can then be combined. The revised database contains the following six relations:

R1(UFN, ULN, HTYPE, HPUR)
R4(CPER, CEXT, CLOC)
R6(SNAME, STYPE)
R8(SNAME, SVER, CPER, SRATE)
R9(UFN, ULN, HPUR, SNAME, SVER, SPUR)
R11(UFN, ULN, ULOC, UDIV, UEXT)

Suppose that a software vendor introduces a new version of a spreadsheet package. The new version is an integrated package that also contains database, wordprocessing and graphics capabilities. The dependency SNAME → STYPE is no longer valid since STYPE is determined by both SNAME and SVER. Relation R6 should be modified as follows:

R12(SNAME, SVER, STYPE)

Relations R8 and R12 can now be combined:

R13(SNAME, SVER, STYPE, SRATE, CPER)

The database now appears as follows:

R1(UFN, ULN, HPUR, HTYPE)
R4(CPER, CLOC, CEXT)
R9(UFN, ULN, HPUR, SNAME, SVER, SPUR)
R11(UFN, ULN, ULOC, UDIV, UEXT)
R13(SNAME, SVER, STYPE, SRATE, CPER)

One other modification may be desirable. To simplify physical implementation, the two key attributes UFN and ULN can be replaced by a single attribute, such as UPER. Key attributes SNAME and SVER can also be replaced by a single attribute SNV. These modifications require the following changes:

Change R11 to R15(UPER, ULOC, UDIV, UEXT).
Change R13 to R16(SNV, STYPE, SRATE, CPER).
Change R1 to R17(UPER, HPUR, HTYPE).
Change R9 to R18(UPER, SNV, HPUR, SPUR).

The final database contains R4, R15, R16, R17 and R18. Two additional relations could be created to capture the detailed SNV and HPER information:

R19(SNV, SNAME, SVER)
R20(UPER, UFN, ULN)

## 3.5 GUIDELINES FOR DEVELOPING RELATIONS IN THIRD NORMAL FORM

Relations in third normal form can be developed by following the guidelines presented in Fig. 3.4. Experienced database designers may find that the problems associated with first or second normal form are obvious. Thus the actual design process may not follow a sequential consideration of all three normal forms; an experienced designer may develop initial relations in third normal form.

1. Define the attributes.
2. Group logically related attributes into relations.
3. Identify candidate keys for each relation.
4. Select a primary key for each relation.
5. Identify and remove repeating groups.
6. Combine relations with identical keys (first normal form).
7. Identify all functional dependencies.
8. Decompose relations such that each nonkey attribute is dependent on all the attributes in the key.
9. Combine relations with identical primary keys (second normal form).
10. Identify all transitive dependencies.
    a. Check relations for dependencies of one nonkey attribute with another nonkey attribute.
    b. Check for dependencies within each primary key (i.e., dependence of one attribute in the key on other attributes within the key).
11. Decompose relations such that there are no transitive dependencies.
12. Combine relations with identical primary keys (third normal form) if no transitive dependencies occur.

**Figure 3.4** Guidelines to develop relations in third normal form.

Third normal form does not eliminate all insertion and deletion problems, and thus more advanced normal forms have been developed. A discussion of these advanced normal forms begins in the next chapter.

## Summary

To avoid future update problems, relations must be carefully constructed. The attributes and primary key must be selected to eliminate repeating groups (first normal form), functional dependencies that involve only part of the primary key (second normal form) and transitive dependencies (third normal form). Examples and guidelines assist in developing relations in third normal form.

## Exercises

3.1   The following two dependencies were listed in the discussion of first normal form:

$$TIME = f(CNUM)$$
$$BLDG = f(CNUM)$$

What assumption about classes is necessary for these dependencies to be valid?

3.2   Suppose that students' names were added to the database:

SMAJ(SNUM, MAJDEPT)
MDEPT(MAJDEPT, COLLEGE)

A new relation, STU(SNUM, SNAME), would be created. This relation has the same key as SMAJ. The process of combining relations with identical primary keys will produce a new relation, STU(SNUM, SNAME, MAJDEPT). What assumption is required so that no transitive dependency exists in the relation STU(SNUM, SNAME, MAJDEPT)?

3.3   Consider the following relation: INV(PNUM, INVENTORY, RESERVE) where

PNUM = part number
INVENTORY = total inventory level
RESERVE = reserve for a future order

An instance of this relation is:

| PNUM | INVENTORY | RESERVE |
|------|-----------|---------|
| 1005 | 10,000    | 3,000   |
| 1008 | 5,000     | 2,000   |
| 2065 | 8,000     | 1,000   |
| 3091 | 5,000     | 3,000   |
| 4069 | 7,000     | 4,000   |

a. Is this relation in first, second or third normal form? Explain your answer.

b. The arithmetic difference between INVENTORY and RE-SERVE is another attribute called AVAILABLE FOR SALE. If this attribute was added to the INV relation, would the resulting relation be in first, second or third normal form? Explain your answer.

3.4 Consider the following five attributes:

SSN       Employee social security number
MAJOR     Major field of study
DEGREE    Degree granted
SCODE     School code
SNAME     School name

and the following two functional dependencies:

$$\text{SSNUM, MAJOR, DEGREE} \rightarrow \text{SCODE}$$
$$\text{SCODE} \rightarrow \text{SNAME}$$

The following relations are in third normal form:

R1(SSNUM, MAJOR, DEGREE, SCODE)
R2(SSNUM, MAJOR, DEGREE, SNAME)

a. What update problems may occur with this decomposition?

b. Suggest a decomposition that will eliminate these problems.

3.5 Given dependencies $A \rightarrow B$, $A \rightarrow C$ and $B \rightarrow C$, relation R(A, B, C) is not in third normal form because of the transitive dependency created by $B \rightarrow C$. Suppose that $C \rightarrow B$ was added to the dependency structure. Would relation R(A, B, C) now be in third normal form? What dependency added to $A \rightarrow B$, $A \rightarrow C$ and $B \rightarrow C$ will guarantee that the single relation R(A, B, C) is in third normal form?

3.6 Given relational schema R(A, B), A → B and B → A,
   a. Is A a candidate key? Explain your answer.
   b. Is B a candidate key? Explain your answer.
   c. Is relation R in third normal form? Explain your answer.

3.7 Given relational schema R(A, B, C), A → B and B → C,
   a. Is A a candidate key? Explain your answer.
   b. Is B a candidate key? Explain your answer.
   c. Is C a candidate key? Explain your answer.

3.8 Given relation R(A, B, C),
   a. Does AB → C? Explain your answer.
   b. Does A → C? Explain your answer.
   c. Does A → B? Explain your answer.

3.9 Given relational schema R(A, B, C), C → B, is the relation in third normal form? Explain your answer.

3.10 Consider relation SUPPLIER(NAME, ADDRESS, PART, PRICE).
   a. What is a primary key for this relation?
   b. Identify a redundancy problem with this relation.
   c. What type of insertion and deletion problems may arise?
   d. Develop an improved database design.

3.11 Given relational schema R(A, B, C, D), BC → D, is the relation in third normal form? Explain your answer.

3.12 Given relational schema R(A, B, C, D), CD → B, is the relation in third normal form? Explain your answer.

3.13 Given relational schema R(A, B, C, D), B → C, B → D and B → A, is the relation in third normal form? Explain your answer.

3.14 Consider relational schema R(A, B, C, D), A → B and ABC → D. Explain why this schema is incorrect.

# Chapter 4

# Boyce-Codd and Fourth Normal Forms

Boyce-Codd normal form and fourth normal form are discussed in this chapter. These advanced normal forms provide additional techniques for eliminating update anomalies. An additional dependency structure, called multivalued, is also introduced.

## 4.1 BOYCE-CODD NORMAL FORM

Recall that a superkey is any set of attributes in a relation that functionally implies every attribute in the relation. Thus a superkey is any set of attributes that contains no duplicate rows in a valid instance of the relation. A candidate key is any superkey such that no other superkey exists that contains fewer attributes.

A relation in first normal form is in **Boyce-Codd normal form** if whenever $X \to A$ and A does not belong to X, then X is a superkey.

For example, relation R in the schema R($\underline{A}$, $\underline{B}$, C), $C \to A$ is in third normal form since A is a member of a candidate key (the primary key). Relation R is not in Boyce-Codd normal form since C is not a superkey.

Boyce-Codd normal form will eliminate some anomalies not addressed by third normal form. Consider the following instance of the relation SCHEDULE(<u>CAMPUS</u>, <u>COURSE</u>, <u>SECTION</u>, TIME, ROOM/BLDG):

| CAMPUS | COURSE | SECTION | TIME | ROOM/BLDG |
|--------|--------|---------|------|-----------|
| East | English 101 | 1 | 8:00 – 9:00 | 212 AYE |
| East | English 101 | 2 | 10:00 – 11:00 | 305 RFK |
| West | English 101 | 3 | 8:00 – 9:00 | 102 PPR |

The relation is in third normal form. No two buildings on any of the university's campuses, however, have the same abbreviation. Thus ROOM/BLDG → CAMPUS and the relation is not in Boyce-Codd normal form. The relation should be decomposed into the following two relations, each in Boyce-Codd normal form:

R1(CAMPUS, COURSE, SECTION, TIME)
R2(ROOM/BLDG, CAMPUS)

Data concerning the availability of a new or remodeled building can then be entered before courses are assigned to that building.

## 4.2 DETERMINANT GROUPS

The set of attributes X in the functional dependency X → A is called the **determinant group** for the dependency.

Boyce-Codd normal form requires that the determinant group for all dependencies X → A (for which A does not belong to X) is a superkey. Note that the values of an instance of a determinant group need not be unique. For example, B is the determinant group for the dependency B → C in the following instance. The values in the instance, however, are not unique in B.

| A | B | C |
|----|----|---|
| 10 | 5 | 2 |
| 15 | 10 | 5 |
| 17 | 20 | 5 |
| 20 | 10 | 5 |

## 4.3 MULTIVALUED DEPENDENCY

The functional and transitive dependency structure can be extended to cover another type of dependency. Consider the relation R(X, Y, Z).

The set X **multivalue determines** the set Y if whenever a valid instance of R(X, Y, Z) contains a pair of rows that contain duplicate values in X, then the instance also contains the pair of rows obtained by interchanging the Y rows in the original pair.

For example, consider the following instance of relation R(X, Y, Z):

| X | Y | Z |
|---|---|---|
| 1 | 1 | 1 |
| 1 | 2 | 2 |
| 1 | 2 | 1 |
| 1 | 1 | 2 |
| 2 | 2 | 2 |

The values in attribute Y can be interchanged in any pair of rows containing identical values in X without creating a row that is not in the instance.

The notation X ⟶⟶ Y is used to indicate that X multivalue determines Y. In a relation R(X, Y), with only two attributes, the multivalued dependency X ⟶⟶ Y always holds. Interchanging the Y values in a pair of rows with identical values in X simply creates the same pair of rows. Thus multivalued dependencies are trivial if a relation contains only two attributes.

A multivalued dependency exists if one set of attributes is dependent on only one other set of attributes in the relation. Thus, in a relation with at least three sets of attributes, a multivalued dependency exists between two sets of attributes (say X and Y) if the values of Y depend only on the value of X, regardless of the values of the other attributes in the relation.

A multivalued dependency may hold within a subset of attributes but not in the entire relation. Consider the relation R(X, Y, Z). Let V be a subset of Z. If Y is multivalued dependent on X in the relation R1(X, Y, V), then Y is said to be **multivalued dependent on X in the context of V**. This is denoted as X ⟶⟶ Y/V. The rightmost notation (/V) is often omitted if the multivalued dependency holds for the entire relation R(X, Y, Z).

### Example 4.1: Multivalued Dependency

Suppose that a relation contains three attributes pertaining to an employee's identification number, work skills and hobbies:

INFO(EMPID, SKILLS, HOBBIES)

This relation is in Boyce-Codd normal form since there are no functional dependencies. An instance of the relation is:

| EMPID | SKILLS | HOBBIES |
|-------|--------|---------|
| 1 | Programming | Golf |
| 1 | Programming | Bowling |
| 1 | Analysis | Golf |
| 1 | Analysis | Bowling |
| 2 | Analysis | Golf |
| 2 | Analysis | Gardening |
| 2 | Management | Golf |
| 2 | Management | Gardening |

The relation is difficult to maintain since adding a new hobby requires multiple new rows corresponding to each skill. This problem is created by the pair of multivalued dependencies EMPID↠SKILLS and EMPID↠HOBBIES. A much better alternative is to decompose INFO into two relations:

SKILLS(EMPID, SKILLS)
HOBBIES(EMPID, HOBBIES)

Multivalued dependencies can occur when the attributes within a relation are not logically related to each other (such as SKILLS and HOBBIES). Many multivalued dependency problems can be avoided by developing relations composed of logically related attributes. Multivalued dependencies can also arise, however, in a special relation that is used to create valid joins. This situation is discussed in the next chapter.

Consider the relation R(A, B, C). The multivalued dependency A↠B implies that for each pair of rows that have the same A value, the corresponding B values can be interchanged without creating any extra rows. Since this is true, it must also be true that interchanging the corresponding C values does not create any extra rows. Therefore, if A↠B, then A↠C also. Thus multivalued dependencies occur in pairs.

## 4.4 INFERENCE AXIOMS FOR MULTIVALUED DEPENDENCIES

A set of inference axioms for functional dependencies was presented in Chapter 2. Figure 4.1 contains a similar set of inference axioms for multivalued dependencies developed by C. Berri, R. Fagin and J. H. Howard ("A Complete Axiomatization for Functional and Multivalued Dependencies in Database Relations," *Proceedings, 1977 ACM SIGMOD International Conference on Management of Data*, Toronto, August 1977).

Note that if $X \twoheadrightarrow Y$ and $X \twoheadrightarrow Z$, then (by axioms 3 and 4) $X \twoheadrightarrow Y \cap Z$, $X \twoheadrightarrow YZ$ and $X \twoheadrightarrow (Y - Z)$.

Two types of trivial multivalued dependencies also exist. A set of attributes will always multivalue imply any of its subsets. For example, $XY \twoheadrightarrow X$ and $XY \twoheadrightarrow Y$. This is similar to the trivial dependencies that occur with functional dependencies. The trivial multivalued dependency occurs since if duplicate rows occur in $XY$, then the values within the subset can always be interchanged (since the subset values are also duplicates).

A second trivial multivalued dependency is $X \twoheadrightarrow (R - X)$, where $R$ includes all the attributes in a relation and $X$ is a subset of these attributes. For example, consider the relation $R(A, B, C)$. The following multivalued dependencies are trivially true:

$$A \twoheadrightarrow BC$$
$$B \twoheadrightarrow AC$$
$$C \twoheadrightarrow AB$$
$$AB \twoheadrightarrow C$$
$$AC \twoheadrightarrow B$$
$$BC \twoheadrightarrow A$$

| | | |
|---|---|---|
| 1. | Reflexive rule | $X \twoheadrightarrow X$ |
| 2. | Augmentation rule | If $X \twoheadrightarrow Y$, then $XZ \twoheadrightarrow Y$. |
| 3. | Union rule | If $X \twoheadrightarrow Y$ and $X \twoheadrightarrow Z$, then $X \twoheadrightarrow YZ$. |
| 4. | Decomposition rule | If $X \twoheadrightarrow Y$ and $X \twoheadrightarrow Z$, then $X \twoheadrightarrow Y \cap Z$ and $X \twoheadrightarrow (Y - Z)$. |
| 5. | Transitivity rule | If $X \twoheadrightarrow Y$ and $Y \twoheadrightarrow Z$, then $X \twoheadrightarrow (Z - Y)$. |
| 6. | Pseudotransitivity rule | If $X \twoheadrightarrow Y$ and $YW \twoheadrightarrow Z$, then $XW \twoheadrightarrow (Z - YW)$. |
| 7. | Complement rule | If $X \twoheadrightarrow Y$ and $Z = R - XY$, then $X \twoheadrightarrow Z$. |

The following axioms, combining functional dependencies and multivalued dependencies, are also true:

8. If $X \rightarrow Y$, then $X \twoheadrightarrow Y$.
9. If $X \twoheadrightarrow Y$ and $Z \twoheadrightarrow W$ (where $W$ is contained in $Y$ and $Y \cap Z$ is not empty), then $X \rightarrow W$.

**Figure 4.1** Inference axioms for multivalued dependencies.

## 4.5 FOURTH NORMAL FORM

A relation in Boyce-Codd normal form will contain no anomalies regarding functional or transitive dependencies. Fourth normal form extends the process to eliminate anomalies associated with multivalued dependencies. These anomalies concern the insertion or deletion of several rows to accommodate a single change in data. An example is provided by the previously discussed attributes EMPID, SKILLS and HOBBIES.

A relation is in **fourth normal form** if the implying set X of
every nontrivial multivalued dependency $X \twoheadrightarrow Y$ is a superkey.

If a nontrivial multivalued dependency exists $(X \twoheadrightarrow Y)$ and X is not a superkey, then the relation is not in fourth normal form. Fourth normal form thus considers some additional dependencies (multivalued dependencies) not addressed by Boyce-Codd normal form.

A relation in Boyce-Codd normal form will also be in fourth normal form unless a multivalued dependency exists for which the determinant group is not a superkey. In this case, the implying set of attributes in the multivalued dependency cannot be an implying set in a functional dependency since the relation is in Boyce-Codd normal form.

For example, consider the relational schema $R(\underline{A}, \underline{B}, \underline{C})$, $B \twoheadrightarrow C$. This relation is in Boyce-Codd normal form since no functional dependencies exist. The relation is not in fourth normal form, however, since attribute B is not a superkey.

## 4.6 ALL-TO-ALL RELATIONSHIPS

Multivalued dependencies are often difficult to recognize. One example of a multivalued dependency is a relationship sometimes referred to as an "all-to-all" relationship. Suppose that a database consists of marketing information regarding competitors. The following rules are in effect:

- Each company sells many products. The same product may be sold by many companies (i.e., product $\twoheadrightarrow$ company and company $\twoheadrightarrow$ product).
- Each company may have many store locations. Many companies may have a store in the same location (i.e., company $\twoheadrightarrow$ location and location $\twoheadrightarrow$ company).

- Each company sells all of its products in all stores. Thus all combinations of products and locations are valid for a given company. This implies that company → product and company → location.

An example illustrating an instance from this relationship is presented in Fig. 4.2. Various insertion and deletion difficulties are associated with this relation. For example, suppose that Northern Ohio Computer Inc. begins selling laser printer #52. Three new rows, corresponding to the three store locations, must be added to the database:

| | | |
|---|---|---|
| Northern Ohio Computer Inc. | Laser printer #52 | Cleveland |
| Northern Ohio Computer Inc. | Laser printer #52 | Canton |
| Northern Ohio Computer Inc. | Laser printer #52 | Akron |

| COMPANY | PRODUCT | LOCATION |
|---|---|---|
| International Computer Inc. | Color monitor #3201 | Los Angeles |
| International Computer Inc. | Color monitor #3201 | Detroit |
| International Computer Inc. | Color monitor #3201 | Cleveland |
| International Computer Inc. | Hard disk #7715 | Los Angeles |
| International Computer Inc. | Hard disk #7715 | Detroit |
| International Computer Inc. | Hard disk #7715 | Cleveland |
| International Computer Inc. | Laser printer #52 | Los Angeles |
| International Computer Inc. | Laser printer #52 | Detroit |
| International Computer Inc. | Laser printer #52 | Cleveland |
| International Computer Inc. | Spreadsheet 4-5-6 | Los Angeles |
| International Computer Inc. | Spreadsheet 4-5-6 | Detroit |
| International Computer Inc. | Spreadsheet 4-5-6 | Cleveland |
| Northern Ohio Computer Inc. | Color monitor #3201 | Cleveland |
| Northern Ohio Computer Inc. | Color monitor #3201 | Canton |
| Northern Ohio Computer Inc. | Color monitor #3201 | Akron |
| Northern Ohio Computer Inc. | Hard disk #7715 | Cleveland |
| Northern Ohio Computer Inc. | Hard disk #7715 | Canton |
| Northern Ohio Computer Inc. | Hard disk #7715 | Akron |
| Northern Ohio Computer Inc. | Database 602 | Cleveland |
| Northern Ohio Computer Inc. | Database 602 | Canton |
| Northern Ohio Computer Inc. | Database 602 | Akron |

**Figure 4.2** An instance of an "all-to-all" relationship.

Four new rows must be added if International Computer Inc. opens a new store in Boston:

International Computer Inc.     Color monitor #3201    Boston
International Computer Inc.     Hard disk #7715        Boston
International Computer Inc.     Laser printer #52      Boston
International Computer Inc.     Spreadsheet 4-5-6      Boston

The same types of problems occur with deletions. The data can be represented in fourth normal form by decomposing the relation into two relations:

PRODUCT(COMPANY, PRODUCT)
STORE(COMPANY, LOCATION)

The instances of these relations corresponding to the data in Fig. 4.2 are presented in Fig. 4.3.

| COMPANY | PRODUCT |
| --- | --- |
| International Computer Inc. | Color monitor #3201 |
| International Computer Inc | Hard disk #7715 |
| International Computer Inc. | Laser printer #52 |
| International Computer Inc. | Spreadsheet 4-5-6 |
| Northern Ohio Computer Inc. | Color monitor #3201 |
| Northern Ohio Computer Inc. | Hard disk #7715 |
| Northern Ohio Computer Inc. | Database 602 |

| COMPANY | LOCATION |
| --- | --- |
| International Computer Inc. | Los Angeles |
| International Computer Inc. | Detroit |
| International Computer Inc. | Cleveland |
| Northern Ohio Computer Inc. | Cleveland |
| Northern Ohio Computer Inc. | Canton |
| Northern Ohio Computer Inc. | Akron |

Figure 4.3 Instances corresponding to the product and store relations.

The data in the two relations is identical to the original data, but including both relations eliminates potential update problems. This also illustrates the way the normalization process can actually reduce the total number of rows in the database.

Note the special type of "many-to-many" relationship defined in this example. For a given company, the product is sold not just at many stores but at all stores. Furthermore, a store sells not just many products but all products. Nothing in the PRODUCT or STORE relations, however, indicates that a product from International Computer Inc. must be sold in the Los Angeles, Detroit and Cleveland stores. No indication is given that the Detroit store must sell color monitor #3201, hard disk #7715, laser printer #52 and spreadsheet 4-5-6, although the two relations can be joined to create the correct information. The join operation is defined in the next chapter.

## Summary

Boyce-Codd normal form and fourth normal form eliminate update anomalies not addressed by third normal form. Boyce-Codd normal form is a logical extension of third normal form. Fourth normal form is concerned with an advanced dependency structure involving multivalued dependencies.

## Exercises

4.1 Given relational schema $R(\underline{A}, B, C, D)$, $B \rightarrow C$ and the following instance:

| A | B | C | D |
|---|---|---|---|
| 1 | 1 | 1 | 1 |
| 2 | 1 | 1 | 1 |
| 3 | 2 | 2 | 2 |
| 4 | 3 | 2 | 3 |
| 5 | 4 | 3 | 3 |
| 6 | 4 | 3 | 4 |

a. Is this instance valid? Explain your answer.
b. Is the relation in third normal form? Explain your answer.
c. Is the relation in Boyce-Codd normal form? Explain your answer.

4.2   Consider this instance of relation R(A, B, C):

| A | B | C |
|---|---|---|
| 1 | 1 | 1 |
| 1 | 1 | 2 |
| 1 | 1 | 3 |
| 2 | 2 | 3 |
| 2 | 3 | 3 |

a. Is this a valid instance of relational schema
   $R(A, \underline{B}, \underline{C})$, $A \twoheadrightarrow B$? Explain your answer.
b. Is this a valid instance of relational schema
   $R(A, \underline{B}, \underline{C})$, $B \twoheadrightarrow C$? Explain your answer.
c. Is this a valid instance of relational schema
   $R(A, \underline{B}, \underline{C})$, $C \twoheadrightarrow A$? Explain your answer.
d. Is this a valid instance of relational schema
   $R(A, \underline{B}, \underline{C})$, $C \twoheadrightarrow B$? Explain your answer.
e. Is this a valid instance of relational schema
   $R(\underline{A}, B, C)$, $BC \twoheadrightarrow A$? Explain your answer.
f. Is this a valid instance of relational schema
   $R(\underline{A}, \underline{B}, C)$, $AB \twoheadrightarrow C$? Explain your answer.

4.3   Consider schema $R(\underline{A}, \underline{B}, C)$, $C \twoheadrightarrow A$.

a. Is the relation in Boyce-Codd normal form? Prove your
   answer.
b. Give a valid instance in which at least two rows contain
   duplicate values for the attribute C.
c. Is the relation in fourth normal form? Prove your answer.

4.4   Consider relation SALESAREA(<u>NUM</u>, CITY, STATE, COM-
      PUTER) and the following instance:

| NUM | CITY | STATE | COMPUTER |
|-----|------|-------|----------|
| 1 | Boston | Massachusetts | IBM |
| 2 | Cleveland | Ohio | Digital |
| 3 | Dallas | Texas | IBM |
| 4 | Buffalo | New York | Univac |
| 5 | Cleveland | Ohio | IBM |
| 6 | Houston | Texas | Digital |

a. Identify an undesirable functional dependency.
b. What are some potential update problems created by this
   functional dependency?
c. How should the undesirable functional dependency be
   eliminated?

**4.5** Given relational schema R(A, B, C, D), A→B, determine which of the following dependencies are implied by the inference axioms discussed in this chapter. State the appropriate axioms if the dependency is implied.

a. A→D
b. C→C
c. AC→B
d. A→BC
e. AC→D

**4.6** Given relational schema R(A, B, C, D), A→B and A→C, determine which of the following dependencies are implied by the inference axioms discussed in this chapter. State the appropriate axioms if the dependency is implied.

a. A→BC
b. AB→C
c. BC→A
d. AC→B
e. B→D

**4.7** Given relational schema R(A, B, C, D, E), A→BC and A→CD, determine which of the following dependencies are implied by the inference axioms discussed in this chapter. State the appropriate axioms if the dependency is implied.

a. A→C
b. A→B
c. A→D
d. A→E
e. A→BCD

**4.8** Given relational schema R(A, B, C, D, E), A→BC and BC→BD, determine which of the following dependencies are implied by the inference axioms discussed in this chapter. State the appropriate axioms if the dependency is implied.

a. A→D
b. A→B
c. AE→BC
d. A→BCD
e. C→BD

**4.9** Given relational schema R(A, B, C, D, E), A→B and BC→DE, determine which of the following dependencies are implied by the inference axioms discussed in this chapter. State the appropriate axioms if the dependency is implied.

a. AC→DE
b. A→DE

    c. $ABC \twoheadrightarrow D$

    d. $ABCD \twoheadrightarrow E$

    e. $BD \rightarrow ACE$

**4.10** Given relational schema R(A, B, C, D), $A \twoheadrightarrow B$ and $B \twoheadrightarrow D$, determine which of the following dependencies are implied by the inference axioms discussed in this chapter. State the appropriate axioms if the dependency is implied.

    a. $A \twoheadrightarrow BD$

    b. $A \twoheadrightarrow CD$

    c. $A \twoheadrightarrow D$

    d. $B \twoheadrightarrow AC$

    e. $A \rightarrow BC$

**4.11** Given relational schema R(A, B, C), $A \rightarrow B$, determine which of the following dependencies are implied by the inference axioms discussed in this chapter. State the appropriate axioms if the dependency is implied.

    a. $A \rightarrow C$

    b. $C \rightarrow A$

    c. $A \twoheadrightarrow BC$

    d. $A \twoheadrightarrow B$

    e. $A \twoheadrightarrow C$

**4.12** Given relational schema R(A, B, C, D), $A \twoheadrightarrow BC$ and $D \rightarrow B$, determine which of the following dependencies are implied by the inference axioms discussed in this chapter. State the appropriate axioms if the dependency is implied.

    a. $A \rightarrow B$

    b. $A \twoheadrightarrow B$

    c. $D \twoheadrightarrow AC$

    d. $AD \twoheadrightarrow B$

    e. $A \rightarrow C$

**4.13** Given attributes A, B, C and D, give an instance of at least two rows that satisfies:

    a. $A \twoheadrightarrow B$ and $B \twoheadrightarrow C$

    b. $A \twoheadrightarrow B$ and $B \twoheadrightarrow\!\!\!\rightarrow C$

    c. $A \twoheadrightarrow\!\!\!\rightarrow B$ and $B \twoheadrightarrow C$

    d. $A \twoheadrightarrow\!\!\!\rightarrow B$ and $B \twoheadrightarrow\!\!\!\rightarrow C$

**4.14** Given attributes A, B, C and D, give an instance of at least two rows that satisfies:

    a. $AB \rightarrow C$ and $C \twoheadrightarrow D$

    b. $AB \rightarrow C$ and $C \twoheadrightarrow\!\!\!\rightarrow D$

    c. $AB \twoheadrightarrow C$ and $C \twoheadrightarrow D$

    d. $AB \twoheadrightarrow C$ and $C \twoheadrightarrow\!\!\!\rightarrow D$

    e. $AB \rightarrow C$ and $C \twoheadrightarrow D$ and $AB \twoheadrightarrow\!\!\!\rightarrow D$

**4.15** Given attributes A, B, C and D, give an instance of at least two rows that satisfies:

    a.  A → B and BC ↠ D

    b.  A → B and BC ⤙ D

    c.  A ⤙ B and BC ↠ D

    d.  A ⤙ B and BC ⤙ D

    e.  A → B and BC ↠ D and A ⤙ D

**4.16** Given R(A, B, C, D), X = ABC, Y = BC and Z = AD, determine which of the following are true:

| | | |
|---|---|---|
| a. X → Y | | g. Y ↠ B |
| b. Y → X | | h. Y ↠ Z |
| c. X ↠ Y | | i. Z ↠ Y |
| d. Y ↠ X | | j. X ↠ Z |
| e. B → Y | | k. X → Z |
| f. B ↠ Y | | l. Y → Z |

# Chapter 5

# Lossless Joins and Dependency Preservation

Modification anomalies associated with functional, transitive and multi-valued dependencies are all eliminated with the attainment of fourth normal form. The relational database designer now has an additional consideration: Has the set of normalized relations been designed in a manner that will correctly answer the end user's ad hoc inquiries? This question can be answered affirmatively if the relations can be joined without creating invalid data. This type of join is called a lossless join.

Several examples of valid and invalid joins are presented in this chapter. The lossless join property is formally defined following these examples. Another property of relational database designs called dependency preservation is also discussed.

## 5.1 RELATIONAL JOINS

The join operator is used to combine data from two relations. Two relations may be joined when the relations share at least one common attribute. The join is implemented by considering each row in an instance of each relation. A row in relation R1 is joined to a row in relation R2 when the value of the common attribute(s) is equal in the two relations. The join of two relations is often called a "binary join."

The join of two relations creates a new relation. The notation "R1 x R2" indicates the join of relations R1 and R2. For example, consider the following instances:

| Relation R1 | | | Relation R2 | | |
|---|---|---|---|---|---|
| A | B | C | B | D | E |
| 1 | 5 | 3 | 4 | 7 | 4 |
| 2 | 4 | 5 | 6 | 2 | 3 |
| 8 | 3 | 5 | 5 | 7 | 8 |
| 9 | 3 | 3 | 7 | 2 | 3 |
| 1 | 6 | 5 | 3 | 4 | 2 |
| 5 | 4 | 3 | | | |
| 2 | 7 | 5 | | | |

Note that the instances of R1 and R2 contain the same data values for attribute B. A more interesting example of a join would include different data values in R1 and R2. Data normalization, however, is concerned with decomposing a relation (e.g., R(A, B, C, D, E)) into smaller relations (e.g., R1 and R2). The data values for attribute B in this context will be identical in R1 and R2. The instances of R1 and R2 are projections of the instance of R(A, B, C, D, E) onto the attributes A, B, C and B, D, E, respectively. A projection will not eliminate data values; duplicate rows are removed, but this will not remove a data value from any attribute.

The join of relations R1 and R2 is possible because B is a common attribute. The result of the join is:

| Relation R1 x R2 | | | | |
|---|---|---|---|---|
| A | B | C | D | E |
| 1 | 5 | 3 | 7 | 8 |
| 2 | 4 | 5 | 7 | 4 |
| 8 | 3 | 5 | 4 | 2 |
| 9 | 3 | 3 | 4 | 2 |
| 1 | 6 | 5 | 2 | 3 |
| 5 | 4 | 3 | 7 | 4 |
| 2 | 7 | 5 | 2 | 3 |

The row ( 2 4 5 7 4 ) was formed by joining the row ( 2 4 5 ) from relation R1 to the row ( 4 7 4 ) from relation R2. The two rows were joined since each contained the same value for the common attribute B. The row ( 2 4 5 ) was not joined to the row ( 6 2 3 ) since the values of the common attribute (4 and 6) are not equal.

The relations joined in the preceding example shared exactly one common attribute. However, relations may share multiple common attributes. All of these common attributes must be used in creating a join. For example, the instances of relations R1 and R2 that follow are joined using the common attributes B and C:

| R1 | | | | R2 | | | | R1 x R2 | | | |
|---|---|---|---|---|---|---|---|---|---|---|---|
| **A** | **B** | **C** | | **B** | **C** | **D** | | **A** | **B** | **C** | **D** |
| 6 | 1 | 4 | | 1 | 4 | 9 | | 6 | 1 | 4 | 9 |
| 8 | 1 | 4 | x | 1 | 4 | 2 | = | 6 | 1 | 4 | 2 |
| 5 | 1 | 2 | | 1 | 2 | 1 | | 8 | 1 | 4 | 9 |
| 2 | 7 | 1 | | 7 | 1 | 2 | | 8 | 1 | 4 | 2 |
| | | | | 7 | 1 | 3 | | 5 | 1 | 2 | 1 |
| | | | | | | | | 2 | 7 | 1 | 2 |
| | | | | | | | | 2 | 7 | 1 | 3 |

The row ( 6 1 4 9 ) was formed by joining the row ( 6 1 4 ) from R1 to the row ( 1 4 9 ) from R2. The join was created since the common set of attributes (B and C) contained identical values (1 and 4). The row ( 6 1 4 ) from R1 was not joined to the row ( 1 2 1 ) from R2 since the common attributes did not share identical values—(1 4) in R1 and (1 2) in R2.

The join operation provides a method for reconstructing a relation that was decomposed into two relations during the normalization process. The join of two rows, however, can create a new row that was not a member of the original relation. Thus invalid information can be created during the join process.

A set of relations satisfies the lossless join property if the instances can be joined without creating invalid data (i.e., new rows). The term lossless join may be somewhat confusing. A join that is not lossless will contain extra, invalid rows. A join that is lossless will not contain extra, invalid rows. Thus the term "gainless join" might be more appropriate.

The significance of the lossless join property is illustrated by two examples. The first example demonstrates why an invalid join operation will create invalid information. The second illustrates why an ad hoc inquiry may be impossible to satisfy without the lossless join property even if the relevant information resides in the database.

**Example 5.1:** Incorrect Information Created by an Invalid Join

---

Consider the following six attributes: STUDENT, COURSE, INSTRUCTOR, HOUR, ROOM and GRADE. Assuming that only one section of a class is offered during a semester, the following functional dependencies can be defined for a semester:

| | | |
|---|---|---|
| HOUR, ROOM | → | COURSE |
| COURSE, STUDENT | → | GRADE |
| INSTRUCTOR, HOUR | → | ROOM |
| COURSE | → | INSTRUCTOR |
| HOUR, STUDENT | → | ROOM |

An instance of these six attributes is:

| STUDENT | COURSE | INSTRUCTOR | HOUR | ROOM | GRADE |
|---------|--------|------------|------|------|-------|
| Pamboukis | Math 1 | Jenkins | 8:00 | 100 | A |
| Chen | English | Goldman | 8:00 | 200 | B |
| Patel | English | Goldman | 8:00 | 200 | C |
| Anderson | Algebra | Jenkins | 9:00 | 400 | A |

The following four relations (each in fourth normal form) can be generated from the given and implied dependencies:

> R1 (STUDENT, HOUR, COURSE)
> R2 (STUDENT, COURSE, GRADE)·
> R3 (COURSE, INSTRUCTOR)
> R4 (INSTRUCTOR, HOUR, ROOM)

Note that the dependencies HOUR, ROOM → COURSE and HOUR, STUDENT → ROOM are not explicitly represented in the preceding decomposition. The goal is to develop relations in fourth normal form that can be joined to answer ad hoc inquiries correctly. This goal can be achieved without representing every functional dependency as a relation. Furthermore, many sets of relations may satisfy the goal. A computer program based on the mathematics developed in the Appendix was used to generate 48 different sets of relations. A few of these sets are presented later in this chapter.

The preceding set of relations can be populated as follows:

| R1 | | | R2 | | |
|----|----|----|----|----|----|
| STUDENT | HOUR | COURSE | STUDENT | COURSE | GRADE |
| Pamboukis | 8:00 | Math 1 | Pamboukis | Math 1 | A |
| Chen | 8:00 | English | Chen | English | B |
| Patel | 8:00 | English | Patel | English | C |
| Anderson | 9:00 | Algebra | Anderson | Algebra | A |

| R3 | | R4 | | |
|----|----|----|----|----|
| COURSE | INSTRUCTOR | INSTRUCTOR | HOUR | ROOM |
| Math 1 | Jenkins | Jenkins | 8:00 | 100 |
| English | Goldman | Goldman | 8:00 | 200 |
| Algebra | Jenkins | Jenkins | 9:00 | 400 |

Suppose that a list of courses with the corresponding room numbers is desired. Relations R1 and R4 contain the necessary information and can be joined using the attribute HOUR. The result of the join is:

| STUDENT | COURSE | INSTRUCTOR | HOUR | ROOM |
|---------|--------|------------|------|------|
| Pamboukis | Math 1 | Jenkins | 8:00 | 100 |
| Pamboukis | Math 1 | Goldman | 8:00 | 200 ** |
| Chen | English | Jenkins | 8:00 | 100 ** |
| Chen | English | Goldman | 8:00 | 200 |
| Patel | English | Jenkins | 8:00 | 100 ** |
| Patel | English | Goldman | 8:00 | 200 |
| Anderson | Algebra | Jenkins | 9:00 | 400 |

The join creates invalid information (denoted by **). Pamboukis, Chen and Patel take the same class at the same time from two different instructors in two different rooms. Jenkins (the math instructor) teaches English and Goldman (the English teacher) teaches math. Both instructors teach different courses at the same time.

Another join possibility is R3 and R4 (joined on INSTRUCTOR). The result is:

| COURSE | INSTRUCTOR | HOUR | ROOM |
|--------|------------|------|------|
| Math 1 | Jenkins | 8:00 | 100 |
| Math 1 | Jenkins | 9:00 | 400 ** |
| English | Goldman | 8:00 | 200 |
| Algebra | Jenkins | 8:00 | 100 ** |
| Algebra | Jenkins | 9:00 | 400 |

Incorrect information is again created. For example, Jenkins teaches Math 1 and Algebra simultaneously at both 8:00 and 9:00.

A correct sequence is to join R1 and R3 (using COURSE) and then join the resulting relation with R4 (using both INSTRUCTOR and HOUR). The details are as follows:

**R1 x R3**

| STUDENT | COURSE | INSTRUCTOR | HOUR |
|---------|--------|------------|------|
| Pamboukis | Math 1 | Jenkins | 8:00 |
| Chen | English | Goldman | 8:00 |
| Patel | English | Goldman | 8:00 |
| Anderson | Algebra | Jenkins | 9:00 |

**(R1 x R3) x R4**

| STUDENT | COURSE | INSTRUCTOR | HOUR | ROOM |
|---------|--------|------------|------|------|
| Pamboukis | Math 1 | Jenkins | 8:00 | 100 |
| Chen | English | Goldman | 8:00 | 200 |
| Patel | English | Goldman | 8:00 | 200 |
| Anderson | Algebra | Jenkins | 9:00 | 400 |

Extracting the COURSE and ROOM attributes (and eliminating the duplicate row corresponding to English) yields the desired result:

| COURSE | ROOM |
|--------|------|
| Math 1 | 100 |
| English | 200 |
| Algebra | 400 |

The correct result is obtained since the sequence (R1 x R3) x R4 satisfies the lossless join property.

A relational database in fourth normal form with the lossless join property can be used to answer unanticipated questions. The choice of joins, however, must be evaluated carefully. Many different sequences of joins will recreate an instance of a relation. Some sequences are more desirable since they result in the creation of less invalid data during the join operations.

Suppose that a relation is decomposed using functional and multivalued dependencies. Then at least one sequence of joins on the resulting relations exists that recreates the original instance, with no invalid data created during any of the join operations.

For example, suppose that a list of grades by room number is desired. This question (which was probably not anticipated during database design) can be answered without creating invalid data by either of the following join sequences:

$$R1 \times R3$$
$$(R1 \times R3) \times R2$$
$$((R1 \times R3) \times R2) \times R4$$

or

$$R1 \times R3$$
$$(R1 \times R3) \times R4$$
$$((R1 \times R3) \times R4) \times R2$$

The required information is contained in relations R2 and R4. These relations, however, cannot be joined directly since they have no common attributes. In this case, the solution requires joining all four relations in the database.

**Example 5.2:** Data not Available for an Inquiry

Departmental training requirements and training history were incorporated in a database consisting of the 16 attributes listed in Fig. 5.1. The following dependencies are associated with these attributes:

| | | |
|---|---|---|
| EPNUM | → | EPNAME |
| EPNUM, CLNUM | → | DCLREQ |
| EPNUM, CLNUM | → | DEPSCH |
| EPNUM, CLNUM | → | DEPCP |
| EPNUM, EPSUP | → | DSTART |
| CLNUM | → | CLNAME |
| CLNUM | → | CLDSC |
| CLNUM | → | VENDOR |
| CLNUM | → | HOURS |
| CLNUM | → | PERNUM |
| CLNUM | → | CREDIT |
| CLNUM | → | MEDIA |

The database consisted of the following five relations, all in Boyce-Codd normal form:

R1 (EPNUM, EPNAME)
R2 (EPNUM, EPSUP, DSTART)
R3 (CLNUM, CLNAME, CLDSC, VENDOR, HOURS, PER-NUM, CREDIT, MEDIA)
R4 (EPNUM, CLNUM, DCLREQ, DEPSCH, DEPCP)
R5 (CLNUM, DCLSCH)

Note that an attribute in a relation need not appear in a functional dependency. For example, DCLSCH does not appear in any of the functional dependencies just identified. Such an attribute can be included in a relation in which all the attributes are part of the primary key (i.e., no nonkey attributes exist in the relation).

Relations R2 and R3 cannot be joined losslessly since no common attributes exist in the two relations. This prevents ad hoc inquiries regarding past history of employee and supervisor combinations. For

| 1. EPNAME | Employee name |
|---|---|
| 2. EPNUM | Employee social security number |
| 3. EPSUP | Employee supervisor social security number |
| 4. CLNAME | Training class name |
| 5. CLNUM | Training class number |
| 6. CLDSC | Description of class |
| 7. DCLREQ | Date class is required |
| 8. DCLSCH | Date class is scheduled |
| 9. DEPSCH | Date a particular employee is scheduled |
| 10. DEPCP | Date an employee completes the class |
| 11. DSTART | Date an employee began reporting to a particular supervisor |
| 12. VENDOR | Vendor associated with the class |
| 13. HOURS | Hours required to complete the class |
| 14. PERNUM | Personnel system number used to indicate completion of the course |
| 15. CREDIT | Number of credits associated with the course |
| 16. MEDIA | Media associated with the course |

**Figure 5.1** Attributes in the training requirements database.

ing to a given supervisor in the past year?" cannot be answered. This problem is eliminated if R5 is expanded as follows:

R5 (<u>CLNUM</u>, <u>DCLSCH</u>, <u>EPNUM</u>, <u>EPSUP</u>)

This modification to R5 results in a database that satisfies the lossless join property. This guarantees that problems such as the one just illustrated will not occur. Thus any of the attributes in the database can be joined to answer unanticipated ad hoc queries.

## 5.2 THE "LOSSLESS JOIN" RELATION

The database may require a "lossless join" relation, which is constructed to assure that any ad hoc inquiry can be answered with relational operators. This relation may contain attributes that are not logically related to each other. This occurs because the relation must serve as a bridge between the other relations in the database. For example, the lossless join relation will contain all attributes that appear only on the left side of a functional dependency. Other attributes may also be required, however, in developing the lossless join relation.

Consider relational schema R(A, B, C, D), A → B and C → D. Relations R1(A, B) and R2(C, D) are in fourth normal form. A third relation R3(A, C), however, is required to satisfy the lossless join property. This relation can be used to join attributes B and D. This is accomplished by joining relations R1 and R3 and then joining the result to relation R2. No invalid data is created during these joins. The relation R3(A, C) is the lossless join relation for this database design.

A relation is usually developed by combining attributes about a particular subject or entity. The lossless join relation, however, is developed to represent a relationship among various relations. The lossless join relation may be difficult to populate initially and difficult to maintain—a result of including attributes that are not logically associated with each other.

The attributes within a lossless join relation often contain multivalued dependencies. Consideration of fourth normal form is important in this situation. The lossless join relation can sometimes be decomposed into smaller relations by eliminating the multivalued dependencies. These smaller relations are easier to populate and maintain.

## 5.3 DEFINITION OF LOSSLESS JOINS

Suppose that R1 and R2 are subsets of a relation R such that the union of R1 and R2 is equal to R. Let *r* be any valid instance of the relational schema for R. The relations R1 and R2 will have a lossless join if the number of rows in the join of their projections is equal to the number of rows in *r*. This is true since a binary join of instances of two relations (i.e., R1 and R2) will recreate all of the rows in the instance of the union of the two relations (i.e., R). If the join of R1 and R2 is lossless, then no extra rows are created. Thus no invalid information is created.

The functional dependencies in the relational schema of R may guarantee that the join of two relations in a decomposition of R is lossless. For example, consider the relational schema R(A, B, C, D), BC → D. A valid instance of this schema is:

| A | B | C | D |
|---|---|---|---|
| 1 | 5 | 8 | 9 |
| 6 | 5 | 8 | 9 |
| 2 | 3 | 7 | 4 |

Suppose that R is decomposed into relations R1(A, B, C) and R2(B, C, D). The projections of the preceding instance on R1 and R2 are:

| R1 | | | | R2 | | |
|---|---|---|---|---|---|---|
| **A** | **B** | **C** | | **B** | **C** | **D** |
| 1 | 5 | 8 | | 5 | 8 | 9 |
| 6 | 5 | 8 | | 3 | 7 | 4 |
| 2 | 3 | 7 | | | | |

The join of these projections will reproduce the original instance without any invalid rows. In fact, all valid instances of R will yield projections whose joins are lossless. This is a consequence of the fact that any pair of rows that are identical in BC will also be identical in D. Thus the functional dependency BC → D guarantees that R1 and R2 satisfy the lossless join property.

This condition can be stated formally as follows: The join of relations R1 and R2 will be a lossless join if the intersection of R1 and R2 is nonempty and if either (or both) of the following is true:

$$V \rightarrow (R1 - V)$$
$$V \rightarrow (R2 - V)$$

where:

V is the intersection attributes of R1 and R2
(R1 – V) is the complement of V in R1
(R2 – V) is the complement of V in R2

For example, consider the database

R1(A, B, C, D)
R2(B, E, F)
R3(A, E, G)
R4(A, B, E)

which was generated from the functional dependencies

AB → C
AB → D
BE → F
AE → G

Relations R1, R2 and R3 are used to satisfy the given functional dependencies. Relation R4 is the lossless join relation that is used to correctly join the other relations.

Suppose that attributes C, E and F are to be joined. Relations R1 and R2 contain the required attributes. If R1 and R2 are joined, then

$$
\begin{aligned}
V &= B \\
(R1 - V) &= ACD \\
(R2 - V) &= EF
\end{aligned}
$$

The join is lossless if either or both of the following dependencies is true:

$$
\begin{aligned}
B &\to ACD \\
B &\to EF
\end{aligned}
$$

Neither dependency is true. Thus the join may not be lossless.

Suppose that R4 (the lossless join relation) is joined with R1. Then:

$$
\begin{aligned}
V &= AB \\
(R1 - V) &= CD \\
(R4 - V) &= E
\end{aligned}
$$

The join is lossless if either or both of the following dependencies is true:

$$
\begin{aligned}
AB &\to CD \\
AB &\to E
\end{aligned}
$$

The dependency $AB \to CD$ is true, and thus the join is lossless. The join creates a new relation RNEW1(A, B, C, D, E). Suppose that this relation is joined with R2. Then:

$$
\begin{aligned}
V &= BE \\
(RNEW1 - V) &= ACD \\
(R2 - V) &= F
\end{aligned}
$$

The join is lossless if either or both of the following dependencies is true:

$$
\begin{aligned}
BE &\to ACD \\
BE &\to F
\end{aligned}
$$

The dependency BE Æ F is true, and thus the join is lossless. The sequence of two lossless joins results in a new relation RNEW2(A, B, C, D, E, F), which contains the required information (C E F) and does not contain any invalid information.

The condition just discussed guarantees that two relations can be joined in a lossless manner. A lossless join can result, however, even if the condition is not satisfied. Thus the condition is sufficient but not necessary. This situation will be explored in the next section by considering the relationship between the lossless join property and multivalued dependencies.

## 5.4 LOSSLESS JOINS AND MULTIVALUED DEPENDENCIES

Consider relational schema R(A, B, C, D), BC $\twoheadrightarrow$ D. A valid instance of this schema is:

| A | B | C | D |
|---|---|---|---|
| 1 | 1 | 1 | 1 |
| 1 | 1 | 1 | 2 |
| 2 | 1 | 1 | 1 |
| 2 | 1 | 1 | 2 |

The projections of the preceding instance on R1(A,B,C) and R2(B,C,D) are:

| R1 | | | | R2 | | |
|----|---|---|---|----|---|---|
| A | B | C | | B | C | D |
| 1 | 1 | 1 | | 1 | 1 | 1 |
| 2 | 1 | 1 | | 1 | 1 | 2 |

The join of these projections will yield the original relation. Note that BC $\twoheadrightarrow$ D and BC $\twoheadrightarrow$ A. Thus the condition specified in the last section is not satisfied. However, the resulting join is lossless. The multivalued dependency BC $\twoheadrightarrow$ D is all that is required to guarantee that the projections of all valid instances of R onto R1 and R2 can be joined in a lossless manner.

A multivalued dependency is a necessary and sufficient condition for two relations to be joined losslessly. Thus if either V $\twoheadrightarrow$ (R1 − V) or V $\twoheadrightarrow$ (R2 − V), in the context of ABCD (where V, R1 and R2 are as defined in the previous section), then the join is lossless.

Furthermore, if R1 and R2 can be joined losslessly, then at least one of the multivalued dependencies $V \twoheadrightarrow (R1 - V)$ or $V \twoheadrightarrow (R2 - V)$ must be true. Note that if one of the multivalued dependencies is true, the other must also be true. Recall that multivalued dependencies occur in pairs. Finally, if the lossless join property is not satisfied, then neither of the multivalued dependencies is true.

Consider an instance of relation R1(A, B, C):

| A. | B | C |
|----|---|---|
| 1  | 1 | 1 |
| 1  | 1 | 2 |

This instance satisfies $B \twoheadrightarrow C$ since the values in C can be interchanged without creating invalid data. This occurs because the two rows contain identical values in A. The following instance of another relation R2(A, B, C) does not contain identical values in A:

| A | B | C |
|---|---|---|
| 1 | 1 | 2 |
| 2 | 1 | 1 |

In this instance, $B \twoheadrightarrow C$ and $B \twoheadrightarrow A$ since this is a valid instance and rows ( 1 1 1 ) and ( 2 1 2 ) are missing. Suppose that relation R2 was decomposed into two relations as follows:

| A | B |
|---|---|
| 1 | 1 |
| 2 | 1 |

| B | C |
|---|---|
| 1 | 2 |
| 1 | 1 |

The join of these two relations is:

| A | B | C |
|---|---|------|
| 1 | 1 | 2 |
| 1 | 1 | 1 ** |
| 2 | 1 | 2 ** |
| 2 | 1 | 1 |

Two invalid rows (indicated by **) are created. Thus the join is not lossless. These are the same two invalid rows created by interchanging the values in C in relation R2. This was the basis for determining that $B \twoheadrightarrow C$.

Alternatively, suppose that an instance of relational schema R3(A, B, C), $B \twoheadrightarrow C$ is composed of the following four rows:

| A | B | C |
|---|---|---|
| 1 | 1 | 2 |
| 1 | 1 | 1 |
| 2 | 1 | 2 |
| 2 | 1 | 1 |

This is a valid instance since the values of C can be interchanged within the rows without creating any invalid data. The relation can be decomposed into two relations:

| A | B |
|---|---|
| 1 | 1 |
| 2 | 1 |

| B | C |
|---|---|
| 1 | 1 |
| 1 | 2 |

The join correctly recreates the original relation.

## 5.5 LOSSLESS JOINS OF ATTRIBUTES

The join operator is used with attributes as well as relations. Two attributes can be joined losslessly if a relation containing both attributes can be formed through a sequence of lossless binary joins. For example, consider the following decomposition of the relation R(A, B, C, D):

$$R1(\underline{A}, B)$$
$$R2(\underline{B}, C)$$
$$R3(\underline{C}, D)$$

Attributes A and C can be joined losslessly since R4(A, B, C), which is equal to R1 x R2, is formed by the lossless binary join of R1 and R2. Attributes A and D can also be joined losslessly by the following sequence of lossless binary joins: R1 x R2 x R3. Also, if the two attributes are both in at least one relation of the decomposition, then the attributes are joined losslessly.

## 5.6 NONUNIQUE SOLUTIONS

Many different database designs may exist that satisfy the lossless join property with each relation in Boyce-Codd or fourth normal form. Consider the example discussed earlier that contained the six attributes

COURSE, INSTRUCTOR, HOUR, ROOM, STUDENT and GRADE and
the following functional dependencies:

| | |
|---|---|
| HOUR, ROOM | → COURSE |
| COURSE, STUDENT | → GRADE |
| INSTRUCTOR, HOUR | → ROOM |
| COURSE | → INSTRUCTOR |
| HOUR, STUDENT | → ROOM |

The inference axioms can be used to generate six additional implied
dependencies:

| | |
|---|---|
| HOUR, COURSE | → ROOM |
| HOUR, ROOM | → INSTRUCTOR |
| INSTRUCTOR, HOUR | → COURSE |
| HOUR, STUDENT | → GRADE |
| HOUR, STUDENT | → COURSE |
| HOUR, STUDENT | → INSTRUCTOR |

These functional dependencies will generate at least 48 sets of relations
such that each relation is in Boyce-Codd normal form and each set satisfies
the lossless join property. A few representative examples of these 48 sets
are illustrated in Fig. 5.2. Additional criteria to determine the characteristics of a "good" database design are required. One such criterion is
dependency preservation.

## 5.7 DEPENDENCY PRESERVATION

A decomposition has **dependency preservation** if all of the
original functional dependencies can be implied from the functional dependencies in the relations forming the decomposition.

Consider relation R(A, B, C) and functional dependencies A → B and A
→ C and B → C. Relation R can be decomposed into two relations, R1(A, B)
and R2(B, C), each in third normal form. The decomposition has dependency preservation if the original three dependencies can be implied from
the functional dependencies in R1 and R2. Note that A → B and B → C can
be implied directly from R1 and R2, respectively. Also, A → C can be
implied from R1 and R2 since A → B and B → C imply that A → C by the
transitivity axiom.

R1 (<u>STUDENT</u>, <u>HOUR</u>, INSTRUCTOR, GRADE)
R2 (<u>INSTRUCTOR</u>, <u>HOUR</u>, ROOM)
R3 (<u>HOUR</u>, <u>ROOM</u>, COURSE)

R1 (<u>STUDENT</u>, <u>HOUR</u>, ROOM)
R2 (<u>HOUR</u>, <u>ROOM</u>, COURSE)
R3 (<u>COURSE</u>, INSTRUCTOR)
R4 (<u>STUDENT</u>, <u>COURSE</u>, GRADE)

R1 (<u>STUDENT</u>, <u>HOUR</u>, ROOM, GRADE)
R2 (<u>HOUR</u>, <u>ROOM</u>, COURSE)
R3 (<u>COURSE</u>, INSTRUCTOR)

R1 (<u>STUDENT</u>, <u>HOUR</u>, COURSE)
R2 (<u>STUDENT</u>, <u>COURSE</u>, GRADE)
R3 (<u>COURSE</u>, INSTRUCTOR)
R4 (<u>INSTRUCTOR</u>, <u>HOUR</u>, ROOM)

R1 (<u>STUDENT</u>, <u>HOUR</u>, ROOM, GRADE)
R2 (<u>COURSE</u>, <u>HOUR</u>, ROOM)
R3 (<u>INSTRUCTOR</u>, <u>HOUR</u>, ROOM)

R1 (<u>STUDENT</u>, <u>HOUR</u>, ROOM, GRADE)
R2 (<u>INSTRUCTOR</u>, <u>HOUR</u>, ROOM)
R3 (<u>COURSE</u>, HOUR)
R4 (<u>COURSE</u>, INSTRUCTOR)

**Figure 5.2** Examples of relations in Boyce-Codd normal form with the set satisfying the lossless join property.

Consider the same dependencies with decomposition R1(A, B) and R2(A, C). Functional dependency $B \rightarrow C$ cannot be implied from R1 and R2 since $A \rightarrow B$ and $A \rightarrow C$ do not imply a dependency between B and C. Thus this decomposition does not have dependency preservation.

A relation can always be decomposed into a set of relations, each in third normal form, such that the lossless join property and dependency preservation are obtained. However, the relation cannot always be decomposed into a set of relations, each in Boyce-Codd normal form, with the lossless join property such that dependency preservation is obtained.

For example, relation R($\underline{A}$, $\underline{B}$, C) with functional dependencies AB → C and C → A is already in third normal form. Any decomposition of this relation to Boyce-Codd normal form, however, will eliminate the dependency preservation property. One such decomposition is R1(A, C) and R2(B, C). Functional dependency AB → C cannot be implied by the dependencies in R1 and R2.

The usefulness of dependency preservation was illustrated in Exercise 3.4. The attributes in the exercise were:

| | |
|---|---|
| SSN | Employee social security number |
| MAJOR | Major field of study |
| DEGREE | Degree granted |
| SCODE | School code |
| SNAME | School name |

The following two functional dependencies were identified:

SSNUM, MAJOR, DEGREE → SCODE
SCODE → SNAME

The following relations are in third normal form:

R1(<u>SSNUM, MAJOR, DEGREE</u>, SCODE)
R2(<u>SSNUM, MAJOR, DEGREE</u>, SNAME)

A school code and school name combination cannot be inserted in the database unless an employee has graduated from that school. The SCODE → SNAME dependency has not been preserved. An improved design is:

R1(<u>SSNUM, MAJOR, DEGREE</u>, SCODE)
R2(<u>SCODE</u>, SNAME)

The SCODE → SNAME dependency is now preserved, eliminating the update problem.

Practical update problems will generally be reduced with dependency preservation. However, the reduction of update problems is not guaranteed. For example, consider dependencies A → B, A → C and B → C. Decomposition R1(A, B) and R2(B, C) preserves all of the dependencies but does not allow direct updates of AC combinations.

## 5.8 FOREIGN KEYS

A **foreign key** is an attribute that appears as a nonkey attribute in one relation and as a primary key (or part of a primary key) in another relation.

Foreign keys may be necessary to correctly join the various relations within the database. Two relations will have a lossless join if a foreign key is the primary key for one of the relations.

For example, consider the decomposition of relation R(A, B, C, D) into three relations R1($\underline{A}$, B), R2($\underline{B}$, C) and R3($\underline{C}$, D). Attribute B is a foreign key in R1, and attribute C is a foreign key in R2. Relations R1 and R2 satisfy the lossless join property since common attribute B is a primary key for R2. The join of R1 and R2 can be joined to R3 since common attribute C is a primary key for R3.

Dependency preservation may be achieved by using foreign keys. For example, consider the school code and school name example discussed in the preceding section. SCODE is a foreign key in R1 and is used to preserve the SCODE $\rightarrow$ SNAME dependency.

Consider the six dependencies A $\rightarrow$ B, A $\rightarrow$ C, A $\rightarrow$ D, B $\rightarrow$ C, B $\rightarrow$ D and C $\rightarrow$ D. The following four decompositions all satisfy the lossless join property, with each relation in Boyce-Codd normal form:

1. R1($\underline{A}$, B)
   R2($\underline{A}$, C)
   R3($\underline{A}$, D)
2. R1($\underline{A}$, B)
   R2($\underline{A}$, D)
   R3($\underline{B}$, C)
3. R1($\underline{A}$, B)
   R2($\underline{B}$, C)
   R3($\underline{B}$, D)
4. R1($\underline{A}$, B)
   R2($\underline{B}$, C)
   R3($\underline{C}$, D)

Decomposition 1 contains no foreign keys. Three dependencies are not preserved: B $\rightarrow$ C, B $\rightarrow$ D and C $\rightarrow$ D. Decomposition 2 contains one foreign key (attribute B). The decomposition is not dependency preserving but only two dependencies are lost: C $\rightarrow$ D and B $\rightarrow$ D. Decomposition 3 contains one foreign key (attribute B), which appears in all three relations.

Only one dependency is lost: $C \rightarrow D$. Finally, decomposition 4 contains two foreign keys (attributes B and C) and is dependency preserving. The number of dependencies lost is nearly inversely proportional to the number of foreign keys.

## 5.9 SEMANTIC DISINTEGRITY

Semantic disintegrity refers to undesirable results that can occur with the use of relational database query languages. Essentially, semantic disintegrity exists when joins are created without the lossless join property. Semantic disintegrity is especially interesting since a study of it approaches the subject of lossless joins in a different context.

A "mapping" from attribute A to attribute B is called one-to-one if $A \rightarrow$ B. Note that the same value of B could map into different values of A. Thus this mapping is not equivalent to a one-to-one mapping in the mathematical sense. The mapping is called one-to-many if $A \twoheadrightarrow B$.

A sequence of mappings must satisfy the lossless join property in order to avoid semantic disintegrity. For example, mapping $A \twoheadrightarrow B$, $B \rightarrow C$ and $C \rightarrow D$, considered in conjunction with relations R1(A, B), R2(B, C) and R3(C, D), implies that relations R1 and R2 will be joined using attribute B and the resulting relation joined with R3 using attribute C.

The first join is valid if B (the intersection of R1 and R2) implies either attribute A (which is R1 − B) or attribute C (which is R2 − B). This join is valid since $B \rightarrow C$. The new relation R(A, B, C) must then be joined to R3 using attribute C. This join is valid if C (the intersection of R and R3) implies either attributes A and B (which is R − C) or attribute D (which is R3 − C). This join is valid since $C \rightarrow D$. Thus the entire mapping is valid, and semantic disintegrity will not occur.

The sequence of joins R1(A, B) to R2(B, C) and the result to R3(C, D) can be used in conjunction with numerous mappings to determine whether semantic disintegrity is a problem. Figure 5.3 illustrates representative examples in which semantic disintegrity problems will not occur.

**Example 5.3:** Valid Joins

Consider again the illustration using the six attributes COURSE, INSTRUCTOR, HOUR, ROOM, STUDENT and GRADE. One decomposition satisfying the lossless join property with each relation in Boyce-Codd normal form is:

1. All mappings are one-to-one (e.g., A → B and B → C and C → D).
2. The only one-to-many mapping is the first mapping in the sequence (e.g., A ↠ B and B → C and C → D).
3. The only one-to-many mapping is the second mapping in the sequence (e.g., A → B and B ↠ C and C → D), but B → A.
4. The only one-to-many mapping is the second mapping in the sequence (e.g., A → B and B ↠ C and C → D), but B ↠ C/A or B ↠ A/C.
5. In cases in which multiple one-to-many mappings exist, the rules for satisfying a lossless join must be examined. The following are representative examples:

   - Mapping: A → B and B ↠ C and C ↠ D
     Requirements:  B ↠ A/C and C ↠ AB/D
                       or B ↠ A/C and C ↠ D/AB
   - Mapping: A ↠ B and B → C and C ↠ D
     Requirements:  C ↠ AB/D or C ↠ D/AB
   - Mapping: A ↠ B and B ↠ C and C ↠ D
     Requirements:  B ↠ A/C and C ↠ AB/D
                       or B ↠ C/A and C ↠ AB/D
                       or B ↠ A/C and C ↠ D/AB
                       or B ↠ C/A and C ↠ D/AB

**Figure 5.3**  Examples in which semantic disintegrity will not occur.

R1(STUDENT, HOUR, ROOM)
R2(HOUR, ROOM, COURSE)
R3(HOUR, ROOM, INSTRUCTOR)
R4(STUDENT, COURSE, GRADE)

A few examples of valid joins are:

| DESIRED RESULT | SEQUENCE OF JOINS |
|---|---|
| INSTRUCTOR and GRADE | ((R1 x R2) x R3) x R4 |
| INSTRUCTOR and COURSE | R2 x R3 |
| GRADE and ROOM | (R1 x R2) x R4 |
| INSTRUCTOR, COURSE and STUDENT | (R1 x R2) x R3 |

Suppose that R1 is removed from the decomposition. The following two pairs of relations can no longer be joined losslessly:

R2 and R4
R3 and R4

The following pairs of attributes can no longer be joined losslessly:

HOUR         and STUDENT
HOUR         and GRADE
ROOM         and STUDENT
ROOM         and GRADE
STUDENT      and INSTRUCTOR
INSTRUCTOR and GRADE

Suppose that R2 is removed from the original decomposition. The following two pairs of relations can no longer be joined losslessly:

R1 and R4
R3 and R4

The following pairs of attributes can no longer be joined losslessly:

HOUR         and COURSE
HOUR         and GRADE
ROOM         and COURSE
ROOM         and GRADE
COURSE       and INSTRUCTOR
INSTRUCTOR and GRADE

## Summary

Fourth normal form will eliminate modification anomalies created by undesirable functional, transitive and multivalued dependencies. A set of relations must also satisfy the lossless join property to ensure that invalid information is not created during the join of two relations. Competing sets of relations may exist that satisfy the lossless join property with each relation in Boyce-Codd or fourth normal form. Dependency preservation is one criterion that may be used to select one set of relations among these competing sets.

## Exercises

5.1   Consider the following dependencies:

EMPLOYEE → DEPARTMENT
EMPLOYEE → JOB TITLE
EMPLOYEE → JOB LEVEL
JOB TITLE → JOB LEVEL

Develop a set of relations in Boyce-Codd normal form that satisfy the lossless join property.

5.2   Consider the following instance:

| NAME | ADDRESS | CITY | STATE | ZIPCODE |
|------|---------|------|-------|---------|
| Smith | 400 Elm Street | Cleveland | Ohio | 44114 |
| Jones | 234 Main Street | Cleveland | Ohio | 44109 |
| Jackson | 350 North Avenue | Akron | Ohio | 44313 |

A transitive dependency exists since ZIPCODE → STATE. The transitive dependence can be eliminated by decomposing the relation into two new relations. Consider the following two alternatives:

R1(NAME, ADDRESS, CITY, ZIPCODE)
R2(ZIPCODE, STATE)

R1(NAME, ADDRESS, CITY, STATE)
R2(ZIPCODE, STATE)

Which alternative is more desirable? Give some examples to substantiate your choice.

5.3   Consider the following instance of relation R(A, B, C, D):

| A | B | C | D |
|---|---|---|---|
| 1 | 1 | 1 | 1 |
| 2 | 1 | 2 | 2 |
| 2 | 2 | 3 | 3 |
| 3 | 2 | 3 | 3 |
| 3 | 3 | 3 | 4 |

This relation can be decomposed into three relations with the following projections:

| R1(A | B | C) | | R2(B | D) | | R3(A | D) |
|------|---|----|---|------|---|---|------|---|
| 1 | 1 | 1 | | 1 | 1 | | 1 | 1 |
| 2 | 1 | 2 | | 1 | 2 | | 2 | 2 |
| 2 | 2 | 3 | | 2 | 3 | | 2 | 3 |
| 3 | 2 | 3 | | 3 | 4 | | 3 | 3 |
| 3 | 3 | 3 | | | | | 3 | 4 |

a. Join the projections from R1 and R2. Does the instance of the new relation contain any invalid information? Show the invalid information if any exists.

b. Join the projections from R1 and R3. Does the instance of the new relation contain any invalid information? Show the invalid information if any exists.

c. Join the projections from R2 and R3. Then join the result with the projection from R1. Does the instance of the new relation contain any invalid information? Show the invalid information if any exists.

5.4 Given the following functional dependencies:

$$AB \rightarrow C$$
$$AB \rightarrow D$$
$$BE \rightarrow F$$
$$AE \rightarrow G$$

and the following relations:

$$R1(A, B, C, D)$$
$$R2(B, E, F)$$
$$R3(A, E, G)$$
$$R4(A, B, E)$$

Suppose that attributes C, E and F are to be joined. What sequence of joins will result in lossless joins at each step?

5.5 Given relational schema R(A, B, C, D), A → B and BC → D:

a. Find a decomposition that satisfies the lossless join property with each relation in Boyce-Codd normal form but that is not dependency preserving.

b. Find a decomposition that satisfies the lossless join property with each relation in Boyce-Codd normal form that also is dependency preserving.

5.6 Given relational schema R(A, B, C, D, E), A → B, CD → A, E → C, C → E and BD → C,

    a. Find four different decompositions that satisfy the lossless join property with each relation in Boyce-Codd normal form. At least 16 such decompositions exist.

    b. Find an alternative primary key for each relation in the following two decompositions:

| | |
|---|---|
| R1(A, <u>D</u>, <u>E</u>) | R1(<u>B</u>, <u>D</u>, E) |
| R2(<u>B</u>, <u>D</u>, E) | R2(<u>B</u>, C, <u>D</u>) |
| R3(<u>C</u>, E) | R3(A, <u>C</u>, <u>D</u>) |

5.7 Consider the following instance of R(A, B, C):

| A | B | C |
|---|---|---|
| 1 | 1 | 1 |
| 1 | 1 | 2 |
| 1 | 2 | 2 |
| 2 | 2 | 1 |
| 2 | 1 | 1 |
| 2 | 1 | 2 |

    a. Does this instance violate B ↠ C? Prove your answer.

    b. Does this instance violate B ↠ A? Prove your answer.

    c. What is the projection of the instance on R1 = AB?

    d. What is the projection of the instance on R2 = BC?

    e. What is the join of the projections identified in parts c and d?

    f. Does the join in part e satisfy the lossless join property? Prove your answer.

5.8 Consider the following instance of R(A, B, C):

| A | B | C |
|---|---|---|
| 1 | 1 | 1 |
| 2 | 2 | 2 |
| 2 | 2 | 1 |
| 1 | 2 | 2 |
| 1 | 2 | 1 |
| 2 | 1 | 1 |

    a. What is the projection of the instance on R1 = AB?

    b. What is the projection of the instance on R2 = BC?

    c. What is the join of the projections identified in parts a and b?

    d. Does the join in part c satisfy the lossless join property? Explain your answer.

    e. Does the original instance violate $B \twoheadrightarrow C$? Explain your answer.

    f. Does the original instance violate $B \twoheadrightarrow A$? Explain your answer.

    g. Does the original instance violate $B \rightarrow C$? Explain your answer.

    h. Does the original instance violate $B \rightarrow A$? Explain your answer.

5.9 Given $R(A, B, C, D, E)$, $A \rightarrow B$ and $D \rightarrow E$, find four sequences of joins of the projections on $R1(A, B)$, $R2(A, C, D)$ and $R3(D, E)$ that recreate R but do not create any invalid data during any of the joins.

5.10 Given $R(A, B, C, D, E)$, $A \rightarrow B$ and $B \rightarrow C$ and $CD \rightarrow E$, find four sequences of joins of the projections on $R1(A, B)$, $R2(A, C)$, $R3(A, D)$ and $R4(C, D, E)$ that recreate R but do not create any invalid data during any of the joins.

5.11 Given $R(A, B, C, D, E)$, $D \rightarrow B$ and $AB \rightarrow C$ and $E \rightarrow A$, find six sequences of joins of the projections on $R1(A, C, D)$, $R2(B, D)$, $R3(A,E)$ and $R4(D, E)$ that recreate R but do not create any invalid data during any of the joins.

5.12 Given $R(A, B, C, D, E)$, $A \twoheadrightarrow B/CD$ and $B \rightarrow E$, find two sequences of joins of the projections on $R1(B, E)$, $R2(A, B)$ and $R3(A,C,D)$ that recreate R but do not create any invalid data during any of the joins.

5.13 Given $R(A, B, C, D, E)$, $A \twoheadrightarrow B/C$ and $C \twoheadrightarrow D/AE$ and $AC \rightarrow B$, find five sequences of joins of the projections on $R1(A,B)$, $R2(A,C)$, $R3(C, D)$ and $R4(A, C, E)$ that recreate R but do not create any invalid data during any of the joins.

5.14 Given $R(A, B, C, D, E)$, $C \rightarrow D$ and $C \rightarrow E$ and $A \twoheadrightarrow B/CD$, find two sequences of joins of the projections on $R1(C, D, E)$, $R2(A,B)$ and $R3(A,C)$ that recreate R but do not create any invalid data during any of the joins.

5.15 Given $R(A, B, C, D, E)$, $A \rightarrow D$ and $BC \rightarrow A$ and $C \rightarrow D$, determine which of the preceding dependencies are not preserved in the following relational structures:

    a. R1(A, B, C)
       R2(B, C, D, E)
    b. R1(A, C)
       R2(C, D, E)
       R3(A, B, D)
    c. R1(A, B, E)
       R2(C, E)
       R3(D, E)
       R4(B, C, D)

5.16 Given $R(A, B, C, D, E)$, $A \rightarrow B$ and $B \rightarrow C$ and $A \rightarrow C$ and $DE \rightarrow B$ and $DE \rightarrow C$, determine which of the preceding dependencies are not preserved in the following relational structures:

    a. R1(A, B, C)
       R2(C, D, E)
    b. R1(A, B)
       R2(B, C)
       R3(B, D, E)
    c. R1(A, B, D)
       R2(B, C, D)
       R3(D, E)
       R4(A, D, E)

5.17 Given $R(A, B, C, D, E)$, $A \twoheadrightarrow B/C$ and $CD \twoheadrightarrow B/A$ and $B \rightarrow E$, determine which of the preceding dependencies are not preserved in the following relational structures:

    a. R1(A, C, E)
       R2(A, B, C, D)
    b. R1(A, B, C)
       R2(B, D, E)
    c. R1(A, B, D)
       R2(B, C, D)
       R3(A, C, E)

5.18 Given $R(A, B, C, D, E)$, $A \rightarrow B$ and $B \twoheadrightarrow C/D$ and $DE \rightarrow C$ and $A \twoheadrightarrow C/D$, determine which of the preceding dependencies are not preserved in the following relational structures:

    a. R1(C, D, E)
       R2(A, C, D)
       R3(A, B, C)
    b. R1(B, C, D)
       R2(A, B, E)
    c. R1(A, C, D)
       R2(C, D, E)
       R3(A, B)

5.19 Consider the functional dependencies and database design discussed earlier in Example 3.1:

> SSNUM, DATE → AMOUNT
> SSNUM, DATE → PAYMENT RATING
> SSNUM        → NAME
> SSNUM        → ADDRESS
> SSNUM        → CITY
> SSNUM        → ZIP
> ZIP          → STATE

> R1(SSNUM, DATE, AMOUNT, PAYMENT RATING)
> R2(SSNUM, NAME, ADDRESS, CITY, ZIP)
> R3(ZIP, STATE)

a. Suppose that attributes STATE and AMOUNT are to be joined. What sequence of joins will result in lossless joins at each step?
b. What attributes cannot be joined losslessly with the preceding decomposition?
c. What relations cannot be joined losslessly with the preceding decomposition?
d. What relation must be added to assure that the preceding decomposition satisfies the lossless join property?

5.20 Consider the functional dependencies and database design discussed earlier in Example 3.2:

> NUM, MACNUM  → SETUP
> NUM, MACNUM  → PRORATE
> NUM          → DES
> NUM, IGD     → AMT

> R1(NUM, MACNUM, SETUP, PRORATE)
> R2(NUM, IGD, AMT)
> R3(NUM, DES)

a. Suppose that attributes DES and SETUP are to be joined. What sequence of joins will result in lossless joins at each step?
b. What attributes cannot be joined losslessly with the preceding decomposition?

    c. What relations cannot be joined losslessly with the preceding decomposition?

    d. What relation must be added to assure that the preceding decomposition satisfies the lossless join property?

5.21 Consider the functional dependencies and database design discussed earlier in Example 3.3:

$$UFN, ULN \rightarrow ULOC$$
$$UFN, ULN \rightarrow UDIV$$
$$UFN, ULN \rightarrow UEXT$$
$$CPER \rightarrow CEXT$$
$$CPER \rightarrow CLOC$$
$$SNAME \rightarrow STYPE$$
$$CPER, SNAME, SVER \rightarrow SRATE$$
$$UFN, ULN, HTYPE, SNAME, SVER \rightarrow SPUR$$
$$SNAME, SVER \rightarrow CPER$$

R1(UFN, ULN, HTYPE, HPUR)
R4(CPER, CEXT, CLOC)
R6(SNAME, STYPE)
R8(SNAME, SVER, CPER, SRATE)
R9(UFN, ULN, HTYPE, SNAME, SVER, SPUR)
R11(UFN, ULN, ULOC, UDIV, UEXT)

    a. Suppose that attributes CEXT and STYPE are to be joined. What sequence of joins will result in lossless joins at each step?

    b. What attributes cannot be joined lossessly with the preceding decomposition?

    c. What relations cannot be joined losslessly with the preceding decomposition?

    d. What relation must be added to assure that the preceding decomposition satisfies the lossless join property?

5.22 Consider the functional dependencies discussed in Section 5.6, Nonunique Solutions:

$$HOUR, ROOM \rightarrow COURSE$$
$$COURSE, STUDENT \rightarrow GRADE$$
$$INSTRUCTOR, HOUR \rightarrow ROOM$$
$$COURSE \rightarrow INSTRUCTOR$$
$$HOUR, STUDENT \rightarrow ROOM$$

Determine whether joining the following relations will result in lossless joins and explain your answer:

a. R1(STUDENT, HOUR, INSTRUCTOR, GRADE)
   R2(INSTRUCTOR, HOUR, ROOM)
b. R1(INSTRUCTOR, HOUR, ROOM)
   R2(HOUR, ROOM, COURSE)
c. R1(STUDENT, HOUR, ROOM, GRADE)
   R2(COURSE, HOUR)
d. R1(COURSE, HOUR)
   R2(COURSE, INSTRUCTOR)

# Part II

## Implementing the Basics

Chapters 6, 7 and 8 are concerned with implementing the material presented in the first five chapters. Chapter 6 presents a detailed study about the development of a small database application. The identification of functional and transitive dependencies is stressed. The change in the dependency structure as the database is modified is also examined. Chapter 7 illustrates a more comprehensive Human Resources database. The emphasis is on using relational operators to correctly answer inquiries. Chapter 8 presents guidelines for implementing data normalization in traditional hierarchical and network database environments.

# Chapter 6

# A Case Study in Data Normalization

The process of normalizing data may appear straightforward in textbook examples. The specification of dependencies, the grouping of attributes and the selection of primary keys, however, usually involve several iterations in actual applications. A small but realistic application of the data normalization process is presented in this chapter. The case study documents the thought process (and some of the mistakes) that occurred in developing the database.

## 6.1 DEFINITION OF THE PROBLEM

The required database will be used to track where various manuals are located within a company. The manuals are classified by name, type, number and vendor. The name and department number of each manual owner must be recorded. The price and account number required to charge the cost of the manual are also needed. Figure 6.1 lists the attributes identified initially.

## 6.2 DEVELOPMENT OF A PRELIMINARY DATABASE DESIGN

An initial evaluation of the attributes listed in Fig. 6.1 resulted in the dependency structure presented in Fig. 6.2. The assumptions necessary to develop the functional dependencies include the following:

- Manuals with the same number also have the same title, price and classification.
- Manuals with the same number are supplied by the same vendor (MNUM → VNAME and MNUM → VADDR are implied dependencies).

| | |
|---|---|
| MNUM | Manual number |
| MTITLE | Manual title |
| PRICE | Price of manual |
| CLASS | Classification (e.g., programming, systems, etc.) |
| VNUM | Vendor number |
| VNAME | Vendor name |
| VADDR | Vendor address |
| ONUM | Owner employee identification number |
| OLNAME | Owner last name |
| OFNAME | Owner first name |
| ODEPTNUM | Owner department number |
| OLOC | Owner mailing location |
| ODEPTNAME | Owner department name |
| COPIES | Number of owner copies |
| PEND | Order-pending flag |
| BNUM | Billing number to charge owner's department |

**Figure 6.1** Initial attributes identified in the case study.

- The combination of manual number and owner identification number identifies the number of copies the owner possesses and whether or not the owner has an order pending for the manual.
- Manuals with the same title are in the same class.
- Vendors are uniquely identified by vendor number.
- No two vendors have the same number or address.
- Owners are uniquely identified by owner identification number.
- Departments are uniquely identified by department number.
- Departments with the same name are given the same billing number (ODEPTNUM → BNUM is an implied dependency). Note that the dependencies allow for different departments to be given the same name.

Based on these dependencies, the following design—in Boyce-Codd normal form with the lossless join property—was developed:

```
        MNUM      →   VNAME
        MNUM      →   VADDR
        MNUM      →   VNUM
        MNUM      →   MTITLE
        MNUM      →   PRICE
        MNUM      →   CLASS
   MNUM,ONUM      →   COPIES
   MNUM,ONUM      →   PEND


       MTITLE     →   CLASS


        VNUM      →   VNAME
        VNUM      →   VADDR
       VNAME      →   VADDR


        ONUM      →   OLNAME
        ONUM      →   OFNAME
        ONUM      →   ODEPTNUM
        ONUM      →   OLOC
        ONUM      →   ODEPTNAME
        ONUM      →   BNUM


    ODEPTNUM      →   ODEPTNAME
    ODEPTNUM      →   BNUM
   ODEPTNAME      →   BNUM
```

**Figure 6.2** Initial specification of functional dependencies.

R1(<u>MNUM</u>, <u>ONUM</u>, COPIES, PEND)
R2(<u>MNUM</u>, MTITLE, PRICE, VNUM)
R3(<u>MNUM</u>, CLASS)
R4(<u>VNUM</u>, VNAME)
R5(<u>VNUM</u>, VADDR)
R6(<u>ONUM</u>, OLNAME, OFNAME, ODEPTNUM, OLOC)
R7(<u>ODEPTNUM</u>, ODEPTNAME)
R8(<u>ODEPTNUM</u>, BNUM)

The relation R1 is used as the lossless join relation in this example. The lossless join relation usually contains only primary key attributes. As the example illustrates, however, this is not always necessary.

## 6.3 EVALUATION OF THE PRELIMINARY DATABASE DESIGN

It is clear that a much more intuitive design would result if relations R7(ODEPTNUM, ODEPTNAME) and R8(ODEPTNUM, BNUM) were combined into a single relation R(ODEPTNUM, ODEPTNAME, BNUM). This relation was not created because a transitive dependency would result since ODEPTNAME → BNUM. Further discussion revealed that if ODEPTNAME → ODEPTNUM was added to the dependency specifications, then the transitive dependency between ODEPTNAME and BNUM would be eliminated.

Consider the three original dependencies:

$$ODEPTNUM \rightarrow ODEPTNAME$$
$$ODEPTNUM \rightarrow BNUM$$
$$ODEPTNAME \rightarrow BNUM$$

An instance for this dependency structure is:

| ODEPTNUM | ODEPTNAME | BNUM |
|----------|-----------|------|
| 1 | MIS | 1 |
| 2 | MIS | 1 |
| 3 | Marketing | 1 |
| 4 | Distribution | 2 |

If the additional dependency ODEPTNAME → ODEPTNUM was added, then the MIS department can be associated with only one department number. Thus the example data would require a change such as the following:

| ODEPTNUM | ODEPTNAME | BNUM |
|----------|-----------|------|
| 1 | MIS | 1 |
| 1 | MIS | 1 |
| 3 | Marketing | 1 |
| 4 | Distribution | 2 |

The duplicate row (1 MIS 1) will be removed from the database. This will remove the duplicate in ODEPTNAME, which is the implying attribute in the former transitive dependency ODEPTNAME → BNUM. Thus the dependency is allowed, and the desired relation R(ODEPTNUM, ODEPTNAME, BNUM) can be created.

The proposed dependency ODEPTNAME → ODEPTNUM is valid. Thus apparent transitive dependencies can sometimes be eliminated by carefully examining the specified functional dependencies. Note that ODEPTNAME is now both a candidate key and a superkey. In the same manner, dependency VNAME → VNUM can be added to generate relation R(VNUM, VNAME, VADDR). VNAME is now a candidate key (and therefore a superkey).

If the two dependencies ODEPTNAME → ODEPTNUM and VNAME → VNUM are added, the desired set of relations (in Boyce-Codd normal form with the lossless join property) can be developed:

> R1(MNUM, ONUM, COPIES, PEND)
> R2(MNUM, MTITLE, PRICE, VNUM)
> R3(MNUM, CLASS)
> R4(VNUM, VNAME, VADDR)
> R5(ONUM, OLNAME, OFNAME, ODEPTNUM, OLOC)
> R6(ODEPTNUM, ODEPTNAME, BNUM)

## 6.4 MODIFICATIONS TO THE DATABASE DESIGN

Suppose that an additional attribute, ODSTART (the date an employee begins work in a department), is added to the database. Dependency ONUM, ODEPTNUM → ODSTART is added since the starting date is dependent on both the employee number and the department number. Dependency ONUM → ODEPTNUM is no longer valid, however, since an employee can be associated with many department numbers during his career. Department number is now a repeating group that must be eliminated from R5. Thus the addition of ODSTART requires the following three changes in the dependency structure:

| | | |
|---|---|---|
| Add | ONUM, ODEPTNUM | → ODSTART |
| Delete | ONUM | → ODEPTNUM |
| Delete | ONUM | → ODEPTNAME |

The following relations may now be created:

> R1(MNUM, ONUM, COPIES, PEND)
> R2(MNUM, MTITLE, PRICE, VNAME)
> R3(MNUM, CLASS)
> R4(VNUM, VNAME, VADDR)
> R5(ONUM, OLNAME, OFNAME, OLOC)
> R6(ODEPTNUM, ODEPTNAME, BNUM)
> R7(ONUM, ODEPTNUM, ODSTART)
> R8(MNUM, ONUM, ODEPTNUM)

Relation R8(<u>MNUM, ONUM,</u> ODEPTNUM) was created to preserve the lossless join property. Suppose that attribute ODEPTNUM was not included as part of the relation. Then the number of the department from which the manual was ordered would not be available if an employee transferred to a new department.

Attribute VNAME must be used to join information regarding the manual number (MNUM) and the vendor number (VNUM). Note that VNAME is not part of the primary key in either relation. Any attribute in a relation should be available for use in the join operation. Some relational database systems, however, allow joins to be performed only on primary key attributes.

If necessary, the relational structure could be modified to accommodate the requirement that joins must be performed on primary keys. For example, since MNUM —> VNUM, relation

R2(<u>MNUM,</u> MTITLE, PRICE, VNAME)

can be changed to

R2(<u>MNUM,</u> MTITLE, PRICE, VNUM)

The join of this relation with

R4(<u>VNUM,</u> VNAME, VADDR)

can now be accomplished with VNUM.

## 6.5 FURTHER ANALYSIS

A further review of the dependencies indicated that MNUM $\rightarrow$ VNUM is not valid. For example, it is possible for two vendors to produce the same manual number. Thus the three dependencies

$$MNUM \rightarrow VNUM$$
$$MNUM \rightarrow VNAME$$
$$MNUM \rightarrow VADDR$$

were eliminated.

The database design was changed as follows:

R1(<u>MNUM</u>, <u>ONUM</u>, COPIES, PEND)
R2(<u>MNUM</u>, MTITLE, PRICE)
R3(<u>MNUM</u>, CLASS)
R4(<u>VNUM</u>, VNAME, VADDR)
R5(<u>ONUM</u>, OLNAME, OFNAME, OLOC)
R6(<u>ODEPTNUM</u>, ODEPTNAME, BNUM)
R7(<u>ONUM</u>, <u>ODEPTNUM</u>, ODSTART)
R8(<u>MNUM</u>, <u>VNUM</u>, <u>ONUM</u>, <u>ODEPTNUM</u>)

The set of dependencies associated with the preceding relational structure are summarized in Fig. 6.3. Each of the relations (with the exception of the lossless join relation R8) is used to represent one or more of the given functional dependencies. The relational structure is not dependency preserving, however, since dependencies MTITLE → CLASS and ONUM → BNUM are not preserved.

Note that if a database is dependency preserving, then any nontrivial implied functional dependencies, as well as the specified dependencies, must be preserved. In this example, the only nontrivial implied functional dependency is ONUM, ODEPTNAME → ODSTART, which is preserved.

## 6.6 EPILOGUE

The database design was generated by attempting to capture all relevant functional dependencies. This often results in a structure that is more complicated than necessary. For example, including both MNUM → CLASS and MTITLE→ CLASS unnecessarily complicates the design process. The desired result is to identify CLASS by the numeric attribute MNUM rather than the alphanumeric attribute MTITLE. Generally, only one set of attributes on the left side of a functional dependency is required to identify an attribute on the right side.

The same situation exists with VNUM → VADDR and VNAME → VADDR. Eliminating VNAME → VADDR results in a simpler dependency structure since VNUM is the preferred choice to identify VADDR. Actually, six dependencies can be eliminated:

| | |
|---|---|
| MTITLE | $\rightarrow$ CLASS |
| VNAME | $\rightarrow$ VADDR |
| VNAME | $\rightarrow$ VNUM |
| ONUM | $\rightarrow$ BNUM |
| ODEPTNAME | $\rightarrow$ ODEPTNUM |
| ODEPTNAME | $\rightarrow$ BNUM |

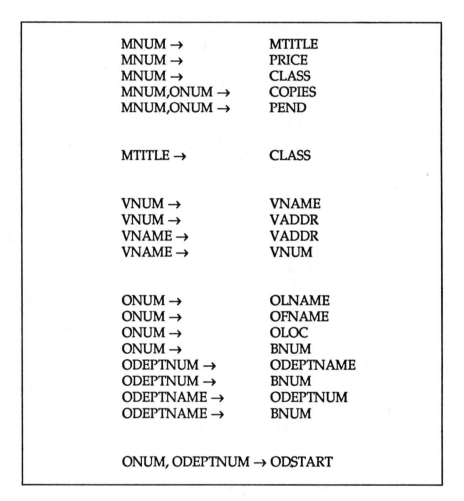

**Figure 6.3** Functional dependencies for the revised database.

This results in a dependency structure with the 13 functional dependencies presented in Fig. 6.4. A relational database design satisfying these functional dependencies with the lossless join property, dependency preservation and each relation in Boyce-Codd normal form is as follows:

R1(<u>MNUM, ONUM</u>, COPIES, PEND)
R2(<u>MNUM</u>, MTITLE, PRICE, CLASS)
R3(<u>VNUM</u>, VNAME, VADDR)
R4(<u>ONUM</u>, OLNAME, OFNAME, OLOC)
R5(<u>ODEPTNUM</u>, BNUM, ODEPTNAME)
R6(<u>ONUM, ODEPTNUM</u>, ODSTART)
R7(<u>MNUM, ONUM, VNUM, ODEPTNUM</u>)

```
 1. MNUM → MTITLE
 2. MNUM → PRICE
 3. MNUM → CLASS
 4. MNUM, ONUM → COPIES
 5. MNUM, ONUM → PEND
 6. VNUM → VNAME
 7. VNUM → VADDR
 8. ONUM → OLNAME
 9. ONUM → OFNAME
10. ONUM → OLOC
11. ODEPTNUM → ODEPTNAME
12. ODEPTNUM → BNUM
13. ONUM, ODEPTNUM → ODSTART
```

**Figure 6.4** Final set of functional dependencies for the case study.

One final modification to the database is necessary. Note that MNUM → VNUM in the context of ONUM and ODEPTNUM in relation R7. This multivalued dependency is recognized since VNUM is not logically related to ONUM or ODEPTNUM. Thus R7 can be decomposed into two relations: R7(MNUM, VNUM) and R8(MNUM, ONUM, ODEPTNUM).

The final database design (in fourth normal form) is:

R1(MNUM, ONUM, COPIES, PEND)
R2(MNUM, MTITLE, PRICE, CLASS)
R3(VNUM, VNAME, VADDR)
R4(ONUM, OLNAME, OFNAME, OLOC)
R5(ODEPTNUM, BNUM, ODEPTNAME)
R6(ONUM, ODEPTNUM, ODSTART)
R7(MNUM, VNUM)
R8(MNUM, ONUM, ODEPTNUM)

## Summary

The dependency structure among attributes is influenced by the end user's perception and use of the data. Consequently correct specification of a dependency structure may require several iterations. The grouping of attributes and the selection of primary keys is also an iterative process. Modifying the database to add or delete attributes may change the dependency structure and result in a new set of iterations.

## Exercises

6.1 Describe what changes in the dependency structure listed in Section 6.5, Further Analysis, would be required to incorporate the following two relations:

R2(<u>MNUM</u>, MTITLE, PRICE)
R3(<u>MNUM</u>, CLASS)

into the following single relation:

R(<u>MNUM</u>, CLASS, MTITLE, PRICE)

Are these changes justified?

6.2 Verify that the design in Section 6.6, Epilogue, is dependency preserving. For example, determine what relation preserves dependency 13. Include any nontrivial implied functional dependencies if such dependencies exist.

6.3 Consider the final database design:

R1(<u>MNUM</u>, <u>ONUM</u>, COPIES, PEND)
R2(<u>MNUM</u>, MTITLE, PRICE, CLASS)
R3(<u>VNUM</u>, VNAME, VADDR)
R4(<u>ONUM</u>, OLNAME, OFNAME, OLOC)
R5(<u>ODEPTNUM</u>, BNUM, ODEPTNAME)
R6(<u>ONUM</u>, <u>ODEPTNUM</u>, ODSTART)
R7(<u>MNUM</u>, <u>VNUM</u>)
R8(<u>MNUM</u>, <u>ONUM</u>, <u>ODEPTNUM</u>)

To satisfy each of the following requirements, determine a sequence of relations to join such that each binary join is lossless and the specified attributes are all in the final joined relation.

a. Join attributes MTITLE and VNAME.
b. Join attributes MTITLE and COPIES.
c. Join attributes ODEPTNAME and VNAME.
d. Join attributes ODSTART and COPIES.
e. Join attributes PRICE and COPIES.
f. Join attributes MTITLE, OLNAME and ODEPTNAME.
g. Join attributes VNAME, COPIES and MNUM.
h. Join attributes ONUM, VNAME and BNUM.

**6.4** Consider the final database design, listed in the preceding exercise. Determine 15 pairs of attributes that cannot be joined losslessly when the specified attribute is removed from R8. Use the fact that since

$$MNUM \twoheadrightarrow VNUM / ONUM, ODEPTNUM$$

then

$$MNUM \twoheadrightarrow VNUM / ONUM$$

and

$$MNUM \twoheadrightarrow VNUM / ODEPTNUM$$

a. Attribute ONUM is removed from R8 (26 such pairs exist).
b. Attribute ODEPTNUM is removed from R8 (36 such pairs exist).

# Chapter 7

# Implementing a Human Resources Database

Implementation of the theory discussed in the first five chapters is continued in this chapter. A new relational operator, selection, is introduced in the context of answering questions regarding a Human Resources database. The database is populated with example data, allowing the results of the join, projection and selection operations to be visualized.

## 7.1 THE SELECTION OPERATOR

The selection operator is used to obtain rows from a database. This operator can be contrasted with the projection operator, which is used to obtain attributes (columns). The selection operator does not play an important role in data normalization theory. The selection operator is critical, however, in implementing queries against the database. Thus knowledge of the selection operator is necessary to understand how normalization theory is implemented.

## 7.2 A TYPICAL QUERY STRUCTURE

The following structure is used in this chapter to illustrate how queries are implementated:

SELECT [attribute 1 (attribute 2 ...)] FROM [relation 1 (relation 2 ...)] WHERE condition where

SELECT   indicates the attributes under consideration
FROM     indicates the required relation(s)
WHERE    indicates the conditions for selecting a set of rows and/
         or the attributes used in the join of two relations.

In this format, SELECT corresponds to the projection operation and WHERE corresponds to the selection operation. The WHERE clause can include the comparison operators

Equal to ( = )
Not equal to ( ≠ )
Greater than ( > )
Greater than or equal to ( ≥ )
Less than ( < )
Less than or equal to ( ≤ )

The WHERE clause can also include one or more of the logical operators OR, AND and NOT.

Typical clauses indicating conditions for selecting a set of rows are:

- Salary is greater than $20,000.
- College degree is equal to master's.
- Department number is not equal to 0003.
- Position number is equal to 006 and sex is equal to female.
- Dependent is equal to husband or dependent is equal to wife.

Suppose that relations R1(A, B, C) and R2(C, D, E) are to be joined to form a new relation with attributes A and E. This can be accomplished with the following statements:

SELECT   A, E
FROM     R1, R2
WHERE    R1.C = R2.C

The WHERE clause indicates that relations R1 and R2 are to be joined using the common attribute C. That is, attribute A from R1 will be combined with attribute E from R2 in all the rows in which the current value of C in R1 is the same as the current value of C in R2.

This structure is patterned after a database sublanguage called SQL (Structured Query Language). SQL is used widely to access data in relational databases. SQL statements may be entered interactively by users at terminals or embedded in applications programs.

Other fourth-generation languages use a similar structure. For example, the preceding join can be accomplished in SAS (Statistical Analysis System) using the statements:

```
DATA RESULT;
MERGE R1 R2;
BY C;
KEEP A E;
```

and in FOCUS (another popular fourth-generation language product) using the statements:

```
JOIN C IN R2 TO C IN R1
TABLE FILE R2
PRINT A E
END
```

## 7.3  THE HUMAN RESOURCES DATABASE

The selection, projection and join operations will be illustrated with a database designed to capture data about employees in a company. The relations will be populated with example data so that the results of relational operations can be visualized. The attributes contained in the Human Resources database are presented in Fig. 7.1.

This example database is concerned with data regarding current employees. Data concerning former employees is assumed to reside in other relations not included in this example. The functional dependencies associated with the attributes are presented in Fig. 7.2. Based on these functional dependencies, the relational database presented in Fig. 7.3 was developed.

| | |
|---|---|
| ADDR | Street address of employee |
| AMT | Amount of pay change |
| BDATE | Birthdate of employee |
| CCODE | Code to describe change in employee status |
| CDATE | Date of change in employee status |
| CDESC | Description of employee status change (CCODE) |
| CITY | City where employee resides |
| CPHONE | Company telephone extension of employee |
| DBDATE | Birth date of employee dependent |
| DEPTNAME | Department name |
| DEPTNUM | Department number |
| DFNAME | First name of employee dependent |
| DLNAME | Last name of employee dependent |
| DSEX | Sex of employee dependent |
| DSSNUM | Social security number of employee dependent |
| ECODE | Education-level code |
| EDATE | Date education level was obtained |
| EDESC | Description of education-level code (ECODE) |
| FNAME | First name of employee |
| HPHONE | Employee home telephone number |
| HR | How-related code (used for dependents) |
| HRDESC | Description of how-related code (HR) |
| LNAME | Last name of employee |
| MNAME | Middle name of employee |
| PAY | Annual pay of employee |
| PLEVEL | Position level |
| PNUM | Position number (unique to each employee) |
| PSUP | Position number of supervisor |
| PTITLE | Position title |
| SCHOOL | School attended |
| SCODE | Education subject code |
| SDESC | Description of education subject code (SCODE) |
| SEX | Sex of employee |
| SSNUM | Social security number of employee |
| STATE | State where employee resides |
| ZIP | Zip code where employee resides |

**Figure 7.1** Attributes in the Human Resources database.

CCODE → CDESC
DEPTNUM → DEPTNAME
DSSNUM → DFNAME
DSSNUM → DBDATE
DSSNUM → DSEX
DSSNUM → DLNAME
ECODE → EDESC
HR → HRDESC
PNUM → PTITLE
PNUM → PLEVEL
PNUM → DEPTNUM
PNUM → PSUP
SCODE → SDESC
SSNUM → ADDR
SSNUM → AMT
SSNUM → FNAME
SSNUM → MNAME
SSNUM → LNAME
SSNUM → BDATE
SSNUM → SEX
SSNUM → CITY
SSNUM → ZIP
SSNUM → HPHONE
SSNUM → CPHONE
SSNUM, CDATE → AMT
SSNUM, CDATE → CCODE
SSNUM, CDATE → PAY
SSNUM, CDATE → PNUM
SSNUM, DSSNUM → HR
SSNUM, SCODE, ECODE, EDATE → SCHOOL
ZIP → STATE

**Figure 7.2** Functional dependencies in the Human Resources database.

```
R1(DEPTNUM, DEPTNAME)
R2(PNUM, PTITLE, PLEVEL, DEPTNUM, PSUP)
R3(SCODE, SDESC)
R4(ECODE, EDESC)
R5(SSNUM, FNAME, MNAME, LNAME, BDATE, SEX, ADDR,
    CITY, ZIP, HPHONE, CPHONE)
R6(SSNUM, DSSNUM, HR)
R7(DSSNUM, DFNAME, DLNAME, DBDATE, DSEX)
R8(SSNUM, CDATE, CCODE, AMT, PAY, PNUM)
R9(HR, HRDESC)
R10(CCODE, CDESC)
R11(SSNUM, SCODE, ECODE, EDATE, SCHOOL)
R12(ZIP, STATE)
```

**Figure 7.3** The Human Resources database.

## 7.4 POPULATION OF THE HUMAN RESOURCES DATABASE

Each of the relations will be populated with realistic data. Only 11 employees will be included so that the results can be verified. The relations are populated in the following figures:

Fig. 7.4    R1(DEPTNUM, DEPTNAME)
Fig. 7.5    R2(PNUM, PTITLE, PLEVEL, DEPTNUM, PSUP)
Fig. 7.6    R3(SCODE, SDESC)
Fig. 7.7    R4(ECODE, EDESC)
Fig. 7.8    R5(SSNUM, FNAME, MNAME, LNAME, BDATE, SEX,
            ADDR, CITY, ZIP, HPHONE, CPHONE)
Fig. 7.9    R6(SSNUM, DSSNUM, HR)
Fig. 7.10   R7(DSSNUM, DFNAME, DLNAME, DBDATE, DSEX)
Fig. 7.11   R8(SSNUM, CDATE, CCODE, AMT, PAY, PNUM)
Fig. 7.12   R9(HR, HRDESC)
Fig. 7.13   R10(CCODE, CDESC)
Fig. 7.14   R11(SSNUM, SCODE, ECODE, EDATE, SCHOOL)
Fig. 7.15   R12(ZIP, STATE)

| DEPTNUM | DEPTNAME |
|---------|----------|
| 0001 | Administration |
| 0002 | Marketing |
| 0003 | Controller |
| 0004 | Manufacturing |
| 0005 | Research |
| 0006 | Purchasing |
| 0007 | Employee Relations |
| 0008 | Management Information Systems |

**Figure 7.4** R1(<u>DEPTNUM</u>, DEPTNAME)

| PNUM | PTITLE | PLEVEL | DEPTNUM | PSUP |
|------|--------|--------|---------|------|
| 001 | President | 50 | 0001 | 001 |
| 002 | Vice president, marketing | 45 | 0002 | 001 |
| 003 | Controller | 45 | 0003 | 001 |
| 004 | Manager, purchasing | 40 | 0006 | 001 |
| 005 | Sales representative | 35 | 0002 | 002 |
| 006 | Secretary, controller | 20 | 0003 | 003 |
| 007 | Accountant | 35 | 0003 | 003 |
| 008 | Director, MIS | 42 | 0003 | 003 |
| 009 | Programmer | 35 | 0003 | 008 |
| 010 | Secretary, purchasing | 20 | 0006 | 004 |
| 011 | Programmer | 35 | 0003 | 008 |

**Figure 7.5** R2(<u>PNUM</u>, PTITLE, PLEVEL, DEPTNUM, PSUP)

| SCODE | SDESC |
|-------|-------|
| Acc | Accounting |
| Mkt | Marketing |
| Mgm | Management |
| Inr | Industrial relations |
| Ier | Industrial engineering |
| Fin | Finance |
| Cpr | College prep |
| Csc | Computer science |

**Figure 7.6** R3(SCODE, SDESC)

| ECODE | EDESC |
|-------|-------|
| Fr | Freshmen (college) |
| Sp | Sophomore (college) |
| Jr | Junior (college) |
| Sr | Senior (college) |
| Hs | High school |
| Ms | Master's |
| Dr | Doctorate |
| Br | Bachelor's |
| Tr | Trade school |

**Figure 7.7** R4(ECODE, EDESC)

| | SSNUM | FNAME | MNAME | LNAME | BDATE | SEX |
|---|---|---|---|---|---|---|
| 1 | 378468921 | Kara | Michelle | Divinski | Dec 6 1946 | F |
| 2 | 897498781 | Mark | Richard | Chibit | Nov 8 1961 | M |
| 3 | 179646391 | Sarah | Stacy | Thomas | Nov 6 1940 | F |
| 4 | 917834981 | Amy | Barbara | Smith | Mar 8 1939 | F |
| 5 | 491874678 | Thomas | Charles | Easterwood | Nov 8 1951 | M |
| 6 | 941637118 | Kim | Erin | Jones | Oct 30 1960 | F |
| 7 | 978748175 | Adam | Josh | Smith | Jan 19 1940 | M |
| 8 | 781619843 | Lauren | Angela | Easterwood | Dec 30 1952 | F |
| 9 | 711984675 | Betsy | Kate | Blair | Jan 6 1941 | F |
| 10 | 765896574 | Vanessa | Martha | Smith | Feb 20 1967 | F |
| 11 | 875496789 | Karen | Cheryl | Brown | Jul 14 1958 | F |

| | ADDR | CITY | ZIP | HPHONE | CPHONE |
|---|---|---|---|---|---|
| 1 | 2465 Maple St. | Fairport Hts. | 93241 | 3452981 | 6678 |
| 2 | 2796 Clarence Rd | Riverside | 94567 | 3457891 | 2391 |
| 3 | 6785 Hill Road | Ocean Park | 93567 | 2578901 | 1070 |
| 4 | 651 School St. | Seaside | 98101 | 3478955 | 3341 |
| 5 | 100 Maple St. | Fairport Hts. | 93241 | 4562981 | 5632 |
| 6 | 846 Dogwood Dr. | Riverside | 94668 | 2671239 | 7568 |
| 7 | 651 School St. | Seaside | 98101 | 3478955 | 9838 |
| 8 | 100 Maple St. | Fairport Hts. | 93241 | 4562981 | 5478 |
| 9 | 26 Northin Rd. | Ocean Park | 93567 | 2312789 | 9897 |
| 10 | 651 School St. | Seaside | 98101 | 3478955 | 2234 |
| 11 | 456 Sharon Dr. | Riverside | 94567 | 5567809 | 1147 |

Numbers at the far left are for reference only and are not part of the database.

**Figure 7.8** R5(<u>SSNUM</u>, FNAME, MNAME, LNAME, BDATE, SEX, ADDR, CITY, ZIP, HPHONE, CPHONE)

| SSNUM | DSSNUM | HR |
|-----------|-----------|---|
| 378468921 | 159711514 | H |
| 378468921 | 967098461 | C |
| 378468921 | 195151200 | C |
| 378468921 | 431186781 | C |
| 378468921 | 431186782 | C |
| 897498781 | 982236786 | W |
| 897498781 | 876009123 | C |
| 179646391 | 198734320 | H |
| 179646391 | 189765490 | C |
| 179646391 | 236578921 | C |
| 179646391 | 567290433 | C |
| 179646391 | 112983786 | C |
| 917834981 | 978748175 | H |
| 917834981 | 765896574 | C |
| 978748175 | 917834981 | W |
| 978748175 | 765896574 | C |
| 491874678 | 781619843 | W |
| 781619843 | 491874678 | H |
| 711984675 | 633328001 | H |
| 875496789 | 733930310 | H |
| 875496789 | 911086334 | C |
| 875496789 | 911987012 | C |
| 875496789 | 913222096 | C |
| 875496789 | 966601843 | C |
| 711984675 | 776381284 | C |
| 711984675 | 798341033 | C |

**Figure 7.9** R6(<u>SSNUM</u>, <u>DSSNUM</u>, HR)

| DSSNUM | DFNAME | DLNAME | DBDATE | DSEX |
|--------|--------|--------|--------|------|
| 159711514 | John | Divinski | Jan 2 1947 | M |
| 967098461 | Ann | Divinski | Mar 13 1978 | F |
| 195151200 | Richard | Divinski | Aug 4 1982 | M |
| 431186781 | William | Divinski | Dec 2 1983 | M |
| 431186782 | Jill | Divinski | Dec 2 1983 | F |
| 982236786 | Jessica | Chibit | Jul 8 1962 | F |
| 876009123 | Lisa | Chibit | Nov 4 1984 | F |
| 198734320 | Charles | Thomas | Oct 7 1942 | M |
| 189765490 | Amy | Thomas | Nov 9 1967 | F |
| 236578921 | Maureen | Thomas | Jan 5 1969 | F |
| 567290433 | Mark | Thomas | Feb 1 1972 | M |
| 112983786 | Karen | Thomas | Apr 5 1973 | F |
| 978748175 | Adam | Smith | Jan 19 1940 | M |
| 765896574 | Vanessa | Smith | Feb 20 1967 | F |
| 917834981 | Amy | Smith | Mar 8 1939 | F |
| 781619843 | Lauren | Easterwood | Dec 30 1952 | F |
| 491874678 | Thomas | Easterwood | Nov 8 1951 | M |
| 633328001 | Richard | Blair | Oct 8 1940 | M |
| 776381284 | Mindy | Blair | Jun 17 1961 | F |
| 798341033 | Henry | Blair | Jun 20 1968 | M |
| 733930310 | Mark | Brown | Dec 4 1958 | M |
| 911086334 | Angela | Brown | Oct 4 1979 | F |
| 911987012 | Thomas | Brown | Jul 6 1981 | M |
| 913222096 | Michael | Brown | Nov 4 1985 | M |
| 966601843 | Katie | Brown | Apr 13 1987 | F |

**Figure 7.10** R7(<u>DSSNUM</u>, DFNAME, DLNAME, DBDATE, DSEX)

| SSNUM | CDATE | | CCODE | AMT | PAY | PNUM |
|---|---|---|---|---|---|---|
| 378468921 | Jun 23 | 1974 | Nh | | 15000 | 107 |
| 378468921 | Jun 1 | 1975 | Mr | 2000 | 17000 | 107 |
| 378468921 | Feb 1 | 1977 | Pr | 4000 | 23000 | 104 |
| 378468921 | Jan 1 | 1978 | Mr | 3000 | 26000 | 104 |
| 378468921 | Mar 15 | 1979 | Pr | 4000 | 30000 | 103 |
| 378468921 | Mar 1 | 1980 | Mr | 3000 | 33000 | 103 |
| 378468921 | Feb 1 | 1984 | Mr | 3000 | 44000 | 103 |
| 378468921 | Mar 1 | 1985 | Mr | 3000 | 47000 | 103 |
| 378468921 | Mar 1 | 1987 | Mr | 4000 | 54000 | 003 |
| 897498781 | Apr 15 | 1984 | Nh | | 28000 | 105 |
| 897498781 | Mar 1 | 1985 | Pr | 4000 | 32000 | 104 |
| 897498781 | Mar 1 | 1987 | Mr | 4000 | 38000 | 004 |
| 179646391 | Aug 15 | 1987 | Nh | | 25000 | 010 |
| 917834981 | Sep 1 | 1980 | Nh | | 17000 | 107 |
| 917834981 | Sep 1 | 1981 | Mr | 1500 | 18500 | 107 |
| 917834981 | Sep 1 | 1984 | Mr | 2000 | 24000 | 107 |
| 917834981 | Sep 1 | 1985 | Mr | 2000 | 26000 | 107 |
| 917834981 | Aug 1 | 1987 | Mr | 3000 | 31000 | 007 |
| 491874678 | Jun 1 | 1985 | Nh | | 24000 | 105 |
| 491874678 | Jun 1 | 1986 | Mr | 4000 | 28000 | 105 |
| 491874678 | Apr 1 | 1987 | Pr | 10000 | 38000 | 002 |
| 941637118 | Jun 1 | 1986 | Nh | | 27000 | 109 |
| 941637118 | Apr 1 | 1987 | Pr | 4000 | 31000 | 008 |
| 978748175 | Jul 1 | 1987 | Nh | | 24000 | 009 |
| 781619843 | Nov 1 | 1985 | Nh | | 17000 | 110 |
| 781619843 | Nov 1 | 1986 | Pr | 3000 | 20000 | 006 |
| 711984675 | Mar 1 | 1976 | Nh | | 20000 | 104 |
| 711984675 | Jun 1 | 1977 | Pr | 4000 | 25000 | 108 |
| 711984675 | Jun 1 | 1978 | Mr | 3000 | 28000 | 108 |
| 711984675 | Apr 1 | 1979 | Pr | 20000 | 48000 | 108 |
| 711984675 | May 1 | 1981 | Pr | 15000 | 67000 | 102 |
| 711984675 | May 1 | 1982 | Mr | 3000 | 70000 | 102 |
| 711984675 | Oct 1 | 1983 | Pr | 5000 | 75000 | 101 |
| 711984675 | Oct 1 | 1984 | Mr | 2000 | 77000 | 101 |
| 711984675 | Oct 1 | 1985 | Mr | 3000 | 80000 | 101 |
| 711984675 | Oct 1 | 1987 | Mr | 5000 | 89000 | 001 |
| 765896574 | Jul 1 | 1987 | Nh | | 18000 | 005 |
| 875496789 | Jul 1 | 1987 | Nh | | 18000 | 011 |

Current position numbers are indicated with a leading zero. Previous positions are indicated with a leading "one." Not all the history was included in this relation. The data was abridged so that the number of rows would be of reasonable size for illustrative purposes.

**Figure 7.11** R8(SSNUM, CDATE, CCODE, AMT, PAY, PNUM)

| HR | HRDESC |
|----|--------|
| H | Husband |
| W | Wife |
| C | Child |

**Figure 7.12** R9(HR, HRDESC)

| CCODE | CDESC |
|-------|-------|
| Nh | New hire |
| Mr | Merit increase |
| Pr | Promotion |

**Figure 7.13** R10(CCODE, CDESC)

| SSNUM | SCODE | ECODE | EDATE | SCHOOL |
|-------|-------|-------|-------|--------|
| 378468921 | Fin | Ms | Jun 1974 | Seaside State University |
| 378468921 | Acc | Br | Jun 1972 | Creek College |
| 897498781 | Ier | Br | Dec 1983 | Riverside University |
| 179646391 | Cpr | Hs | Jun 1958 | Fairport High |
| 917834981 | Acc | Br | Jun 1961 | Fairlawn Business College |
| 491874678 | Mkt | Dr | Apr 1981 | University of Fairport |
| 491874678 | Mgm | Ms | Jun 1976 | University of Fairport |
| 491874678 | Mkt | Br | Jun 1973 | University of Fairport |
| 941637118 | Csc | Br | Jun 1982 | Riverside University |
| 978748175 | Cpr | Hs | Jun 1958 | Fairport High |
| 781619843 | Inr | Jr | Jun 1973 | University of Fairport |
| 711984675 | Acc | Dr | Apr 1970 | Ocean Park University |
| 711984675 | Acc | Ms | Jun 1965 | Ocean Park University |
| 711984675 | Acc | Br | Jun 1963 | Ocean Park University |
| 765896574 | Mkt | Sp | Jun 1987 | Seaside State University |
| 875496789 | Csc | Br | Jun 1980 | Riverside University |

**Figure 7.14** R11(SSNUM, SCODE, ECODE, EDATE, SCHOOL)

| ZIP | STATE |
|-----|-------|
| 98101 | Maryland |
| 93241 | Virginia |
| 94567 | Maryland |
| 94668 | Maryland |
| 93567 | Virginia |

**Figure 7.15** R12(ZIP, STATE)

## 7.5 EXAMPLES OF QUERIES AGAINST THE HUMAN RESOURCES DATABASE

The following examples illustrate how the projection, selection and join operators can be combined to obtain information from the database. After the step-by-step details are given, the steps are combined in one concise SELECT statement.

**Example 7.1**

For all employees with a master's degree, find the name of the employee and the major field of his or her degree.

a. Use the projection operator to select attributes SSNUM and SCODE from R11. Then use the selection operator to find the master's degrees.

```
SELECT   SSNUM, SCODE
FROM     R11
WHERE    ECODE = "Ms"
```

The result is the relation Ra(SSNUM, SCODE) with the following instance:

```
378469821        Fin
491874678        Mgm
711984675        Acc
```

b. Join relation Ra with R5 using SSNUM. Then use the projection operator to select attributes FNAME, MNAME,
LNAME and SCODE.

```
SELECT      FNAME, MNAME, LNAME, SCODE
FROM        R5, Ra
WHERE       R5.SSNUM = Ra.SSNUM
```

The result is the following instance of Rb(FNAME,
MNAME, LNAME, SCODE):

| Kara | Michelle | Divinski | Fin |
|------|----------|----------|-----|
| Thomas | Charles | Easterwood | Mgm |
| Betsy | Kate | Blair | Acc |

c. Join relation Rb with R3 using SCODE. Then use the projection operator to select attributes FNAME, MNAME,
LNAME and SDESC.

```
SELECT      FNAME, MNAME, LNAME, SDESC
FROM        R3, Rb
WHERE       Rb.SCODE = R3.SCODE
```

The result is the following instance of Rc(FNAME, MNAME,
LNAME, SDESC):

| Kara | Michelle | Divinski | Finance |
|------|----------|----------|---------|
| Thomas | Charles | Easterwood | Management |
| Betsy | Kate | Blair | Accounting |

Using SQL, the preceding three steps can be accomplished with one
concise statement:

```
SELECT      FNAME, MNAME, LNAME, SDESC
FROM        R11, R5, R3
WHERE       R11.SSNUM = R5.SSNUM
            AND
            R11.SCODE = R3.SCODE
            AND
            ECODE = "Ms"
```

## Example 7.2

What is the educational background of the director of MIS?

a. Use the selection operator with relation R2 to find the position number of the director of MIS. Then join this result with R8 to find the social security number of the director of MIS.

```
SELECT    PNUM, SSNUM
FROM      R2, R8
WHERE     PTITLE = "Director, MIS"
          AND
          R2.PNUM = R8.PNUM
          AND
          PNUM < 100
```

The result is the following instance of Ra(PNUM, SSNUM):

008    941637118

b. Obtain the educational background by joining relation Ra with R11.

```
SELECT    SCODE, ECODE, EDATE, SCHOOL
FROM      Ra, R11
WHERE     Ra.SSNUM = R11.SSNUM
```

The result is the following instance of Rb(SCODE, ECODE, EDATE, SCHOOL):

Csc    Br    Jun 1982    Riverside University

The preceding steps can be accomplished with one concise statement:

```
SELECT    SCODE, ECODE, EDATE, SCHOOL
FROM      R2, R8, R11
WHERE     PTITLE = "Director, MIS"
          AND
          R2.PNUM ▬ R8.PNUM
          AND
          R8.SSNUM = R11.SSNUM
```

More descriptive information can be obtained by joining Rb with R4 (using ECODE) and R3 (using SCODE). This will result in SDESC replacing SCODE and EDESC replacing ECODE.

Although these two examples appear similar, a major difference exists. In the first example, the join of R11 and R5 is lossless since SSNUM is the intersection of R5 and R11 and SSNUM is also the key for R5. The join of (R11 x R5) with R3 is also lossless since SCODE is the intersection of (R11 x R5) and R3 and SCODE is also the key for R3. Thus no invalid information is created during either of the joins.

The join of R2 and R8 in the second example is lossless since PNUM is the intersection of R2 and R8 and PNUM is also the key for R2. The intersection of R8 and R11 (SSNUM), however, is not the key for either R8 or R11 or R2 x R8. Thus the join of R8 and R11 or (R8 x R2) and R11 may not be lossless.

SSNUM → CDATE, CCODE, PAY, AMT and PNUM, however, in the context of SCODE, ECODE, EDATE and SCHOOL. This is true since, for a given SSNUM, every pair of rows (CDATE, CCODE, PAY, AMT, PNUM) and (SCODE, ECODE, EDATE, SCHOOL) is valid. Thus the join of R8 and R11 is lossless. Furthermore, R2 x (R8 x R11) is also lossless since PNUM is the intersection of (R8 x R11) and R2 and PNUM is also the key of R2.

Consider the join of R11 and R6. SSNUM is the intersection of R11 and R6. Although SSNUM is part of the key for both R11 and R6, SSNUM is not the entire key for either relation. Thus the join of R11 and R6 may not be lossless. SSNUM → DSSNUM, HR, however, in the context of SCODE, ECODE, EDATE and SCHOOL. Thus the join is lossless.

## 7.6 LOSSLESS JOINS AND MULTIVALUED DEPENDENCIES

If no multivalued dependencies existed, then the join of any of the following pairs of relations would not be lossless:

| | | | | | |
|---|---|---|---|---|---|
| R1, R3 | R1, R4 | R1, R6 | R1, R7 | R1, R9 | R1, R11 |
| R2, R3 | R2, R4 | R2, R6 | R2, R7 | R2, R9 | R2, R11 |
| R3, R6 | R3, R7 | R3, R8 | R3, R9 | R3, R10 | |
| R4, R6 | R4, R7 | R4, R8 | R4, R9 | R4, R10 | |
| R6, R8 | R6, R10 | R6, R11 | | | |
| R7, R8 | R7, R10 | R7, R11 | | | |
| R8, R9 | R8, R11 | | | | |
| R9, R10 | R9, R11 | | | | |
| R10, R11 | | | | | |

The addition of a lossless join relation

<u>R13(SSNUM, DSSNUM, CDATE, SCODE, ECODE, EDATE)</u>

would guarantee that the preceding pairs of relations could be joined losslessly. SSNUM → DSSNUM, however, in the context of CDATE, SCODE, ECODE and EDATE. Thus DSSNUM should be removed from R13 and included with SSNUM in a new relation. However, this was already accomplished in R6.

Similarly, SSNUM → CDATE in the context of SCODE, ECODE and EDATE. Thus CDATE should be removed from R13 and included with SSNUM in a new relation. However, this was already accomplished in R8. The remaining attributes in R13 are already contained in R11. Thus the multivalued dependencies have eliminated the need for R13.

The fact that no multivalued dependencies exist in the first 12 relations is easy to verify. In addition, all 12 relations can be joined losslessly in the following sequence:

R6 x R8 x R11 x R3 x R2 x R1 x R4 x R5 x R7 x R9 x R10 x R12

The first two joins, R6 x R8 and (R6 x R8) x R11, are lossless because of the multivalued dependencies just described. The remaining joins are lossless since the intersection of the relations involved in the join is also the key of one of these relations. Thus the database satisfies the lossless join property, and each relation is in fourth normal form.

## 7.7 THE EXISTS OPERATOR

The relational operators join, projection and selection were used to illustrate how queries to the database are answered. Many relational databases contain other operators that are used to facilitate answering other types of questions. For example, suppose that a query was concerned with identifying dependent twin children. This can be accomplished by determining whether duplicate values for DBDATE in R7 are associated with the same SSNUM.

Determining whether duplicate values exist in DBDATE is difficult using the relational operators discussed in this text. A logical operator EXISTS, however, can be used to answer the question. The value of a logical operator is either "true" or "false." A typical query structure would temporarily consider R7 as two relations (e.g., A and B). The EXISTS operator would be included in the WHERE clause as follows:

```
SELECT     DFNAME, DLNAME
FROM       R6, R7
WHERE      EXISTS
               SELECT
               FROM     A, B
               WHERE    R6.SSNUM = R7.SSNUM
                        AND
                        A.DBDATE = B.DBDATE
                        AND
                        A.SSNUM = B.SSNUM
```

This query would determine that William and Jill Divinski are twins. The variety of available relational operators is an important variable in selecting database software. A true relational database system should include capabilities to answer any user query.

## Summary

The projection, selection and join operators are combined to obtain information from the database. These operators are included in fourth generation languages that implement queries against the database. Lossless joins are not created automatically. Specifying the correct relations and the proper sequence of joins is usually the responsibility of the user.

## Exercises

Write SELECT statements to obtain the required information in Exercises 7.1 through 7.14. Show which instance answers the query correctly.

Assume that a date before 1968 can be found by the clause WHERE DATE < Jan 1 1968 and that other dates and comparisons can be expressed similarly. (Most languages include such a capability, although the syntax details may vary.)

7.1   Find the name and current salary of each employee.

7.2   Find the names of employees who live in Virginia.

7.3   Find the names and dates of hire of all current employees hired before 1981

7.4   Find the names and posrtion levels of employees with position level 42 or greater

**7.5**   Find the names of employees who report directly to the controller.

**7.6**   List the home telephone number of each employee living in the city of Ocean Park or holding a doctoral degree.

**7.7**   Find the name and birth date of the wife of each employee in the Controller Department.

**7.8**   Find the names of the children of Betsy Kate Blair.

**7.9**   Find the names of the children of each employee who graduated from the University of Fairport.

**7.10**  Find the name of employee, name of dependent child and birth date of dependent child for each child born before 1968.

**7.11**  Find the names of current employees born before 1945 who were employed by the company before 1983. List name, date of birth and date of hire for each of these employees.

**7.12**  List the name and date of hire for all employees hired in 1985.

**7.13**  List the name and current job title for each employee promoted in 1985.

**7.14**  List the name, date and amount of increase for each employee who received a merit pay increase in 1985.

**7.15**  Prove that R5 x R8 is a lossless join.

**7.16**  Prove that R12 x R5 is a lossless join.

**7.17**  Identify a potential problem in the join (R1 x R2 x R8 x R6 x R7). What multivalued dependency allows this join to be lossless?

**7.18**  Suppose that R1 and R3 are to be joined. What sequence of joins will result in a lossless join at each step?

# Chapter 8

# Implementation of Data Normalization In Traditional Database Environments

Data normalization is usually associated with relational database design. A set of normalized relations can be implemented, however, in traditional hierarchical and network environments. This chapter presents some guidelines for accomplishing this implementation. These guidelines may require modifications to accommodate the requirements of the particular database system in use.

The terminology associated with hierarchical and network structures is not standard. For consistency, the terms attribute and row will continue to be used in this text. A specific vendor's implementation, however, may use different terms.

---

## 8.1 PROBLEM DEFINITION

An example will illustrate how a normalized set of relations can be implemented in hierarchical and network database environments. The example concerns the development of a database to track employees' training requirements and completed courses. The relevant attributes are presented in Fig. 8.1.

The following dependencies were identified:

| | |
|---|---|
| SSNUM | → NAME |
| CNUM | → CDESC |
| CNUM | → CREDITS |
| DNUM | → DNAME |
| SSNUM, CNUM, SDATE | → GRADE |

The same class can be scheduled on different dates, and thus CNUM ↠ DATESCH. An employee can enter, leave and reenter the same department, and thus SSNUM, DNUM ↠ BEGDATE. These relationships may involve multivalued dependencies. A multivalued dependency, however,

| SSNUM | Employee identification number |
| NAME | Employee name |
| CNUM | Number of course |
| CDESC | Description of course |
| CREDITS | Number of course credits |
| DNUM | Employee department number |
| DNAME | Employee department name |
| SDATE | Date employee is scheduled in class (or historical information regarding the date employee participated in class) |
| GRADE | Grade employee received in class |
| DATESCH | Various dates for which class is scheduled |
| BEGDATE | Date employee began work in department |

**Figure 8.1** Attributes in the training requirements database.

is determined in the context of a specific relational structure. Thus no specification of a multivalued dependency can be made at this point.

No functional dependency implies either BEGDATE or DATESCH. This is another clue that BEGDATE and DATESCH may enter into a multivalued dependency. An attribute that is not implied by some set of attributes will be included in a relation that contains only primary key attributes (i.e., no nonkey attributes). This relation often contains multivalued dependencies since the attributes are not logically related to each other.

The functional dependencies were used to develop the following database, which satisfies the lossless join property (each relation is in Boyce-Codd normal form):

STUDENT(<u>SSNUM</u>, NAME)
CLASS(<u>CNUM</u>, CDESC, CREDITS)
DEPT(<u>DNUM</u>, DNAME)
STUCLASS(<u>SSNUM</u>, <u>CNUM</u>, <u>SDATE</u>, GRADE)
LOSSLESS(<u>DNUM</u>, <u>SSNUM</u>, <u>CNUM</u>, <u>BEGDATE</u>, <u>DATESCH</u>,
    <u>SDATE</u>)

Two multivalued dependencies can be identified in the context of the LOSSLESS relation:

CNUM $\twoheadrightarrow$ DATESCH
SSNUM, DNUM $\twoheadrightarrow$ BEGDATE

Thus the LOSSLESS relation can be decomposed into three relations that have a lossless join:

CLASSCHED(<u>CNUM, DATESCH</u>)
DHISTORY(<u>SSNUM, DNUM, BEGDATE</u>)
LOSSLESS2(<u>DNUM, SSNUM, CNUM, SDATE</u>)

Relations STUDENT, CLASS, DEPT, STUCLASS, CLASSCHED, DHISTORY and LOSSLESS2 will be used to illustrate the implementation guidelines.

## 8.2 IMPLEMENTATION IN A HIERARCHICAL ENVIRONMENT

A hierarchical database consists of nodes connected by branches. The top node is called the root. If multiple nodes appear at the top level, the nodes are called root segments. The parent of node $n_i$ is a node directly above $n_i$ and connected to $n_i$ by a branch. Each node (with the exception of the root) has exactly one parent. The child of node $n_i$ is the node directly below $n_i$ and connected to $n_i$ by a branch. One parent may have many children.

By introducing data redundancy, complex network structures can also be represented as hierarchical databases. This redundancy is eliminated in physical implementation by including a "logical child." The logical child contains no data but uses a set of pointers to direct the database management system to the physical child in which the data is actually stored. Associated with a logical child are a physical parent and a logical parent. The logical parent provides an alternative (and possibly more efficient) path to retrieve logical child information.

A set of normalized relations can be modeled in a hierarchical structure by applying the guidelines presented in Fig. 8.2. These guidelines are applied to the relations discussed in the previous section:

R1 STUDENT(<u>SSNUM</u>, NAME)
R2 CLASS(<u>CNUM</u>, CDESC, CREDITS)
R3 DEPT(<u>DNUM</u>, DNAME)
R4 STUCLASS(<u>SSNUM, CNUM, SDATE</u>, GRADE)
R5 CLASSCHED(<u>CNUM, DATESCH</u>)
R6 DHISTORY(<u>SSNUM, DNUM, BEGDATE</u>)
R7 LOSSLESS2(<u>DNUM, SSNUM, CNUM, SDATE</u>)

The application of the guidelines is illustrated in Figs. 8.3 through 8.9. The details are as follows:

1. A relation with a primary key consisting of one attribute is represented as a root segment. Note that, as used in this chapter, the term root segment is associated with a hierarchical database. It is not the same as the root segment discussed in Chapter 10.
2. A relation with a primary key consisting of two attributes is represented in one of the following ways:
   a. If exactly one of the attributes in the key appears as the primary key in a single key relation (root segment), then the relation is represented as a physical child of the root segment identified by the key.
   b. If both the attributes in the key appear as primary keys in single key relations, then the relation is represented as a logical child of the segments identified in the key.
   c. If none of the attributes in the key appear as primary keys in a single-key relation, consider a relation with three or more attributes in the primary key. Apply rule 3, following, and readdress the two key relation when a successful mapping using rule 2a or rule 2b can be accomplished.
3. A relation with a primary key consisting of three or more attributes is represented using the following guideline: The primary key must be segmented into multiple, overlapping two-attribute keys. For example:

RELATION (KEY1, KEY2, KEY3, data)

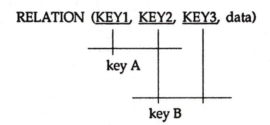

Database segments are identified for the overlapping two-key attributes based on the application of rule 2.

**Figure 8.2** Guidelines for implementation in a hierarchical model.

Figure 8.3:   Relations STUDENT (R1), CLASS (R2) and DEPT (R3) are represented as root segments (guideline 1).

Figure 8.4:   Relation STUCLASS (R4) is represented using guideline 3. Pair SSNUM, CNUM is represented as a logical child of the CLASS and STUDENT root segments (guideline 2b).

Figure 8.5:   CNUM, SDATE and GRADE are represented as a physical child of the SSNUM, CNUM logical child (guideline 3).

Figure 8.6:   Relation CLASSCHED (R5) is represented as the physical child of the CLASS root segment using guideline 2a.

Figure 8.7:   Relation DHISTORY (R6) is represented using guideline 3. Pair SSNUM, DNUM is represented as a logical child of the STUDENT and DEPT root segments (guideline 2b).

Figure 8.8:   Pair DNUM, BEGDATE is represented as a physical child of the logical child containing SSNUM, DNUM (guideline 3).

Figure 8.9:   Relation LOSSLESS2 (R7) is represented using guideline 3. However, pair DNUM, SSNUM is already represented by R6, pair SSNUM, CNUM is already represented by R4 and pair CNUM, SDATE is already represented by R4.

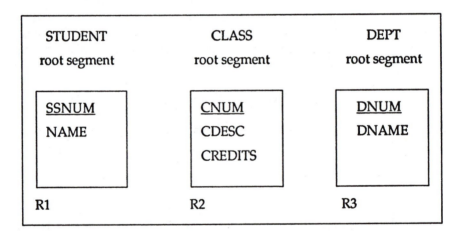

**Figure 8.3** Representation of root segments.

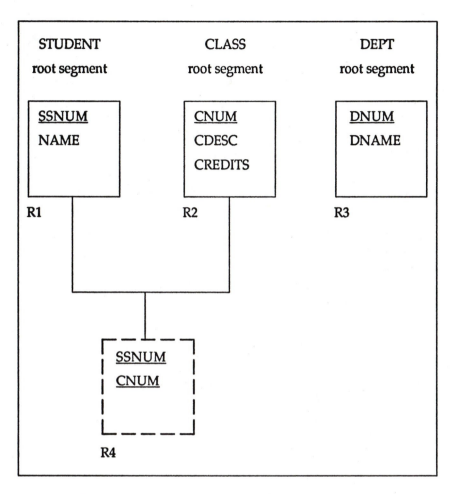

**Figure 8.4** Representation of R4 as a logical child.

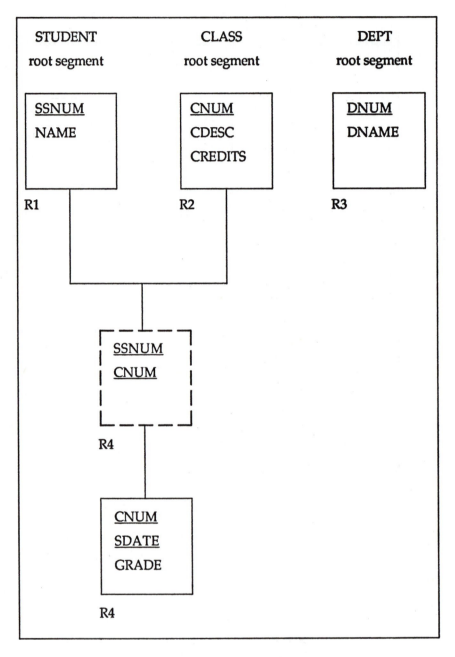

**Figure 8.5** Representation of R4 as a physical child.

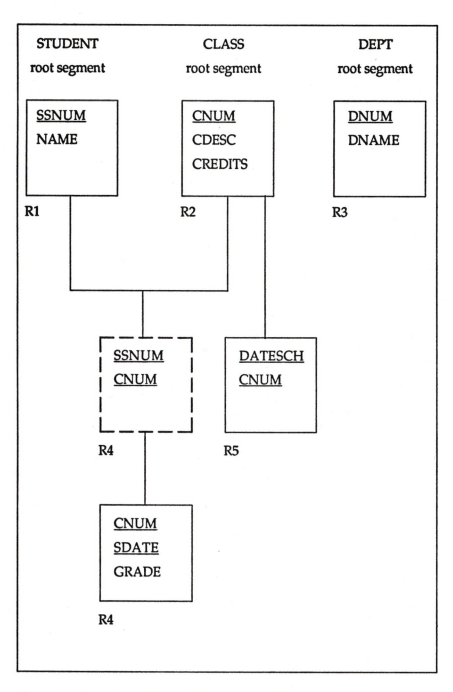

**Figure 8.6** Representation of R5 as a physical child.

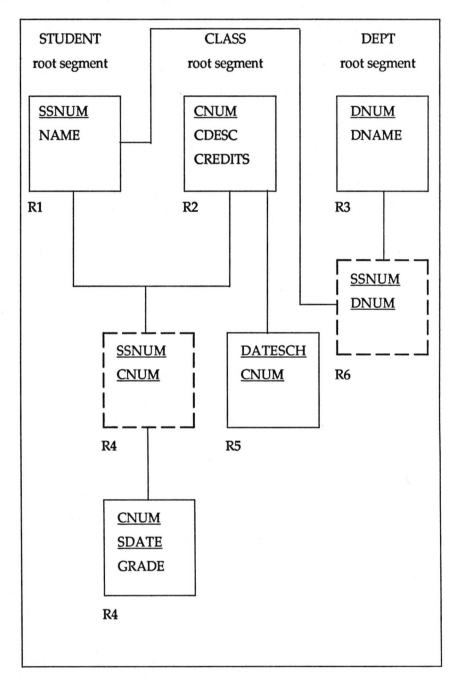

**Figure 8.7** Representation of R6 as a logical child.

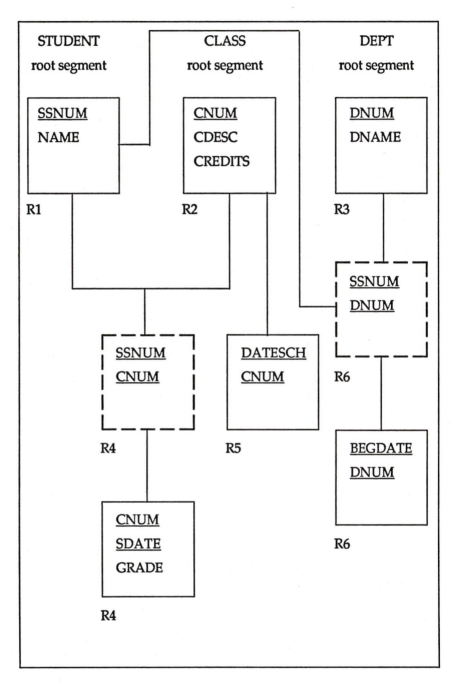

**Figure 8.8** Representation of R6 as a physical child.

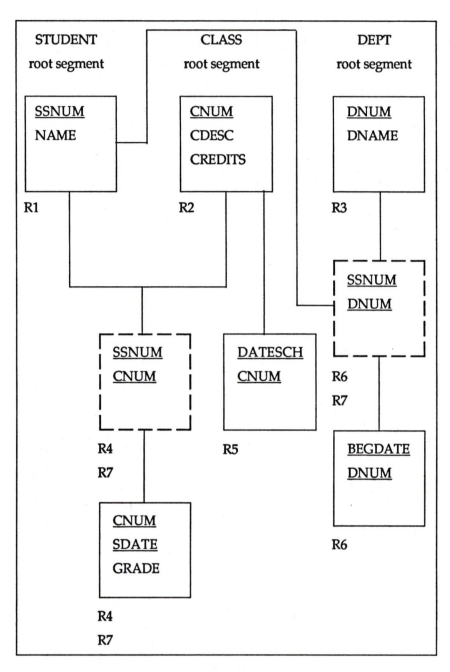

**Figure 8.9** Final hierarchical representation.

The logical relational model assumes that the order of the attributes is of no significance. Attribute order is significant, however, in physical implementation. The guidelines may yield a somewhat different structure if the order of the primary key attributes is changed within a relation.

For example, the preceding implementation resulted from applying the guidelines to R7 LOSSLESS2(<u>DNUM, SSNUM, CNUM, SDATE</u>). If the attributes were reordered to R7 LOSSLESS2(<u>SSNUM, DNUM, CNUM, SDATE</u>), then a DNUM, CNUM logical child would be created. The choice of implementation should be based on the criteria usually employed in designing hierarchical databases (e.g., machine performance, user views etc.).

## 8.3 IMPLEMENTATION IN A NETWORK ENVIRONMENT

A network also consists of nodes and branches. In contrast to the hierarchical structure, however, a child may have multiple parents in the network structure.

The relations discussed in the hierarchical implementation example can be represented as a network by applying the following guidelines:

1. A relation with a single primary key is represented as a root entry in the database.
2. A relation with a primary key consisting of two or more attributes, one or more of which appear as a primary key in a single-key relation (root entry), is represented as a member in sets in which the owners are the root entries.

The application of these guidelines is illustrated in Figures 8.10, 8.11 and 8.12. The details are as follows:

Figure 8.10:  Relations STUDENT (R1), CLASS (R2) and DEPT (R3) are represented as root entries (an application of guideline 1).

Figure 8.11:  Relation CLASSCHED (R5) is represented as a member in a set with the CLASS root entry as the owner (an application of guideline 2).

Figure 8.12:  Relations STUCLASS (R4), DHISTORY (R6) and LOSSLESS2 (R7) are represented as records that are members of the respective set relations STUDENT, CLASS and DEPT.

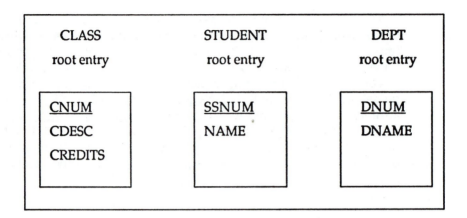

**Figure 8.10** Representation of root entries.

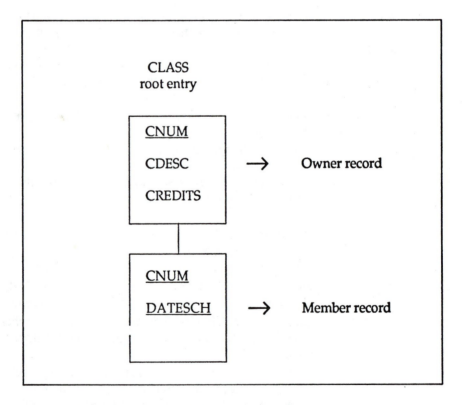

**Figure 8.11** Representation of R5 as a set member.

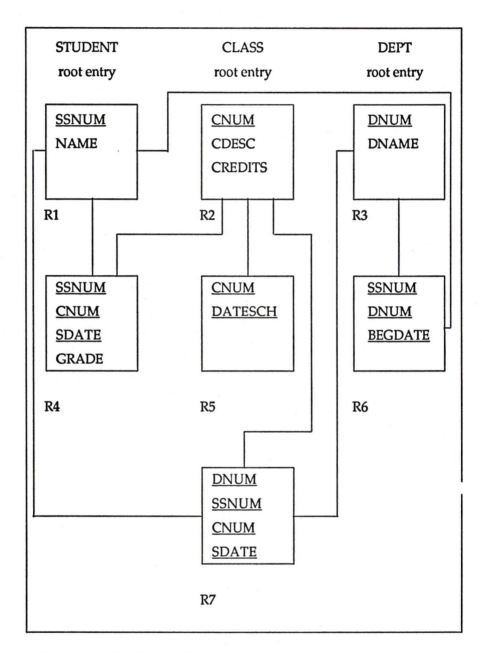

**Figure 8.12** Final network representation.

## Summary

Data normalization is used in logical database design. A normalized set of relations can be implemented physically in relational, hierarchical or network database environments. Guidelines exist for transforming a normalized set of relations into traditional hierarchical or network structures.

## Exercises

8.1   Suppose that the decomposition in Section 8.1 included the STU-DENT, CLASS, DEPT, STUCLASS, CLASSCHED and DHISTORY relations but not the LOSSLESS2 relation. Twenty-two pairs of attributes in the decomposition cannot be joined losslessly without the LOSSLESS2 relation. Find as many of these pairs as you can.

8.2   Consider the following decomposition, based on the attributes discussed in Chapter 6:

R1(MNUM, ONUM, VNUM, ODEPTNUM)
R2(ONUM, ODEPTNUM, ODSTART)
R3(ODEPTNUM, BNUM, ODEPTNAME)
R4(MNUM, ONUM, COPIES, PEND)
R5(VNUM, VNAME, VADDR)
R6(ONUM, OLNAME, OFNAME, OLOC)
R7(MNUM, MTITLE, PRICE, CLASS)

a. Develop a hierarchical model for this decomposition.
b. Develop a network model for this decomposition.

8.3   Consider the following decomposition, based on the attributes discussed in Example 3.3:

R4(CPER, CLOC, CEXT)
R15(UPER, ULOC, UDIV, UEXT)
R16(SNV, STYPE, SRATE, CPER)
R17(UPER, HTYPE, HPUR)
R18(UPER, SNV, HPUR, SPUR)

a. Develop a hierarchical model for this decomposition.
b. Develop a network model for this decomposition.

Note that this database was developed before the lossless join property was discussed.

# Part III

# Advanced Theory

Chapters 9 and 10 and the Appendix, intended for individuals desiring a technical presentation of normalization theory, present a more technically oriented discussion of this theory. The normal forms discussed in Part 1 are presented from a mathematical viewpoint. More advanced material, including additional normal forms, is also presented.

Chapter 9 describes the theory of data normalization as related to primary keys. An additional normal form (domain-key normal form) is defined and illustrated. Advanced data dependencies and fifth normal form are described in Chapter 10. The Appendix contains a more rigorous presentation of normalization theory.

# Chapter 9

# The Role of Keys in Data Normalization

The data normalization theory discussed previously did not directly consider the selection of primary keys. An equivalent theory of normal forms has been developed, however, in which keys are extremely important. This chapter presents data normalization from the perspective of primary keys. Relevant definitions are presented; a series of examples is then used to illustrate the concepts.

## 9.1 CONSTRAINTS

A **constraint** is any limitation that is placed on a relation.

For example, the values of an attribute may be constrained to be less than 100, or equal to either 0 or 1, or nonnegative. Functional dependencies, multivalued dependencies and the lossless join property are also constraints.

## 9.2 BOYCE-CODD NORMAL FORM

A relation in first normal form is in **Boyce-Codd normal form if** the primary key implies all the functional dependencies.

## 9.3  KEY DEPENDENCY

A **key dependency** is a constraint that requires a set of attributes to be a superkey.

Note that the entire set of attributes is always a key dependency. Candidate keys are also key dependencies.

## 9.4  FOURTH NORMAL FORM

A relation is in **fourth normal form** if the set of key dependencies implies all the multivalued dependencies.

This essentially requires that the set of attributes associated with the left side of a functional or multivalued dependency is a superkey.

## 9.5  PROJECTION-JOIN DEPENDENCY

A **projection-join dependency** is a constraint that requires that a set of relations satisfy the lossless join property.

## 9.6  PROJECTION-JOIN NORMAL FORM

A relation is in **projection-join normal form** if the set of key dependencies guarantees that the set of projection-join dependencies is satisfied.

A relation in projection-join normal form is also in fourth normal form (and consequently also in Boyce-Codd normal form and third normal form). This is true since a correspondence exists between projection-join dependencies and multivalued dependencies. A projection-join dependency holds in a relation if and only if a multivalued dependency holds.

Consider relation $R(X, Y, Z)$. The projection-join dependency between $XY$ and $YZ$ holds if and only if $Y \twoheadrightarrow X$. The only way in which key dependencies can imply that a projection-join dependency between XY and YZ holds is if the key dependencies require that Y is a superkey.

Thus key dependencies require that sets of attributes contain no duplicate rows in valid instances. For example, if X is a primary key, then XY is required to be a superkey. Thus, if key dependencies require join dependencies to hold, then the implying set of each of the corresponding multivalued dependencies must be a superkey. This implies that fourth normal form is satisfied.

## 9.7  DOMAIN-KEY NORMAL FORM

A relation is in **domain-key normal form** if all constraints (functional dependencies, multivalued dependencies, projection-join dependencies and any other constraints specified) are implied by the set of key dependencies and the domains of the attributes.

A relation may be in domain-key normal form without being in fourth normal form. This is true since fourth normal form is determined by considering the set of key dependencies, while domain-key normal form considers both the set of key dependencies and the set of domains.

Consider the multivalued dependency $A \twoheadrightarrow B$. This constraint is satisfied if the domain of B contains only one value. Thus multivalued dependencies and functional dependencies can be implied by domains without being implied by the set of key dependencies. If the domain of each attribute on the right side of a functional or multivalued dependency contains more than one value, however, then domain-key normal form does imply fourth normal form.

## 9.8  EXAMPLES

A series of examples is used to illustrate the relationship between primary keys and the definitions of normal forms. In each case, a relation and a set of constraints are given. The appropriate normal form is selected by determining what constraints can be implied by the primary key and the attribute domains.

A few observations concerning primary keys and domains may help clarify the examples. The primary key can sometimes guarantee that a functional dependency and a multivalued dependency hold in a relation.

If K is the primary key of a relation and X is a set of attributes containing K (i.e., K is a subset of X), then X is a superkey. When X is a superkey, then X $\rightarrow$ Y and X $\twoheadrightarrow$ Y hold automatically since no valid instance can exist in which two rows contain identical values in X. For example, consider the relation R($\underline{A}$, B, C, D). Set AB is a superkey since the set contains A. Therefore AB $\rightarrow$ C and also AB $\twoheadrightarrow$ C.

Knowledge of the domain of an attribute can also be used to show that a functional dependency holds. Suppose that the domain of attribute A is just one value (i.e., the values of A in all valid instances of the relation must be identical). Then A is implied by any set X of attributes. This is true since if X $\twoheadrightarrow$ A, then a valid instance of the relation must exist in which two rows contain identical values in X but different values in A. This is not possible if the domain of A is limited to one value.

If the domain of each attribute contains at least two values, then functional dependencies and multivalued dependencies are implied by only the set of keys. Thus the domains do not enter the determination of Boyce-Codd normal form or fourth normal form. Finally, note that a primary key implies a dependency if the key requires that the left side of the dependency is a superkey.

### Example 9.1

---

*Relation:*     R($\underline{A}$, B)

*Constraint:*   A $\rightarrow$ B

*Conclusion:*   The relation is in Boyce-Codd normal form since the constraint can be implied by the primary key. Higher normal forms are not relevant since the relation involves only two attributes, and no constraints on domains are given.

---

### Example 9.2

---

*Relation:*     R($\underline{A}$, B, C)

*Constraint:*   AB $\rightarrow$ C

*Conclusion:*   The relation is in Boyce-Codd normal form since the constraint is satisfied by specifying that A is the primary key. Note that AB is a superkey. The relation would also be in Boyce-Codd normal form if either B or AB was specified as the primary key.

---

### Example 9.3

*Relation:*    R($\underline{A}$, B, C, D)

*Constraint:*   BC → D

*Conclusion:*  The relation may not be in third normal form since the fact that attribute A is the key does not imply that BC is a superkey.

### Example 9.4

*Relation:*    R($\underline{A}$, B, C)

*Constraints:*  B → C
The domain of C is restricted to exactly one value (i.e., the data values for attribute C must be identical).

*Conclusion:*  The constraint B → C is satisfied by the limitation on the domain of attribute C. Whenever all the data values of an attribute must be identical, then that attribute will be implied by all the attributes in the relation. In order for B $\twoheadrightarrow$ C, a valid instance of R($\underline{A}$, B, C) must exist in which two rows contain identical values in B but not identical values in C. This is not possible since the values of C must be identical. The relation is thus in domain-key normal form. Note that the constraint B → C is not implied by the primary key A. A primary key implies a dependency if the determinant group of the dependency contains the primary key.

### Example 9.5

*Relation:*    R(A, B, $\underline{C}$, D)

*Constraints:*  A $\twoheadrightarrow$ B
               BC → D

*Conclusion:*  The constraint BC → D holds since C is a primary key and therefore BC is a superkey. Thus the relation is in Boyce-Codd normal form. The multivalued dependency A $\twoheadrightarrow$ B, however, is not implied by primary key C. The fact that C is a primary key does not require that A must be a superkey. A valid instance of R could exist in which two rows contain identical values in A. Thus the relation may not be in fourth normal form.

## Example 9.6

*Relation:*     R(A, B, C, D)

*Constraints:*  A → B
                BC → D

The domain of B is restricted to exactly one value (i.e., the data values for attribute B must be identical).

*Conclusion:*   The relation is in domain-key normal form since the primary key C and the domain of B imply that both constraints hold. Since C is a primary key, BC is a superkey and thus BC → D. The domain of B, consisting of only one value, guarantees that A → B and therefore A → B. The relation may not be in fourth normal form, however, since the constraint A → B holds but A may not be a superkey. The relation is in Boyce-Codd normal form since BC is a superkey.

## Example 9.7

*Relation:*     R(A, B, C, D)
                where A and B are both candidate keys.

*Constraints:*  AC → D
                BD → C

*Conclusion:*   The relation is in domain-key normal form since both constraints are implied by the set of candidate keys. Candidate key A implies constraint AC → D; candidate key B implies constraint BD → C. The relation is also in Boyce-Codd normal form since the determinant group for each constraint is a superkey.

## Example 9.8

*Relation:*     R(A, B, C)

*Constraint:*   The set of relations { R1(A, B), R2(B, C) } must satisfy the lossless join property.

*Conclusion:*   The relation is in projection-join normal form since B → C or B → A (which must be true since B is a primary key) guarantees that the lossless join property is satisfied.

**Example 9.9**

---

*Relation:*    R(A, <u>B</u>, C, D)

*Constraints:*  B→»C and the set { R1(A, B), R2(B, C),  R3(C, D) } must satisfy the lossless join property.

*Conclusion:*  The relation is in fourth normal form since the dependency B→»C is implied by the primary key. The relation is not in projection-join normal form, however, since the primary key does not guarantee that the join of relations R1, R2 and R3 is lossless.

**Example 9.10**

---

*Relation:*    R(A, <u>B</u>, C, D)

*Constraints:*  The set { R1(A, B), R2(B, C), R3(C, D) } must satisfy the lossless join property. The domain of D is restricted to exactly one value.

*Conclusion:*  The relation is in domain-key normal form since the primary key guarantees that R1(A, B) and R2(B, C) satisfy the lossless join property. The join (A,B,C) and (C,D) also satisfies the lossless join property since the domain of D is restricted to one value. The relation is not in projection-join normal form, however, since the primary key alone (without domain restrictions) does not imply that the join of (A, B, C) and (C, D) is lossless.

## Summary

The theory of data normalization can be developed by considering the role of primary keys and superkeys. This requires expanding the dependency structure among attributes to include key dependencies and projection-join dependencies. Two additional normal forms—projection-join normal form and domain-key normal form—are considered in this regard.

## Exercises

9.1  *Given:* R(<u>A</u>, B, C)

*Constraint:* A → B

a. Is relation R in third normal form? Prove your answer.
b. Is relation R in Boyce-Codd normal form? Prove your answer.

**9.2**  *Given:* R($\underline{A}$, B, C)

Constraints: A → B and B → C

  **a.** Is relation R in third normal form? Prove your answer.
  **b.** Is relation R in Boyce-Codd normal form? Prove your answer.
  **c.** Can a relation in Boyce-Codd normal form not be in third normal form? Explain your answer.

**9.3**  *Given:* R($\underline{A}$, B, $\underline{C}$)

Constraint: A → B

  **a.** Is relation R in third normal form? Prove your answer.
  **b.** Does AC → B? Prove your answer.

**9.4**  *Given:* R($\underline{A}$, $\underline{B}$, C)

Constraint: BC → A

  **a.** Is relation R in third normal form? Prove your answer.
  **b.** Is relation R in Boyce-Codd normal form? Prove your answer.
  **c.** Is BC a candidate key? Prove your answer.

**9.5**  *Given:* R($\underline{A}$, B, C, D)

Constraint: AB → C

  **a.** Is relation R in third normal form? Prove your answer.
  **b.** Is relation R in Boyce-Codd normal form? Prove your answer.
  **c.** Does AB ↠ C? Prove your answer.
  **d.** Does the set { R1(A, B, C), R2(A, B, D) } satisfy the lossless join property? Explain your answer.

**9.6**  *Given:* R(A, B, C, D)

Constraints: A → B

  B → C

  C → D

  **a.** Does A → D? Prove your answer.
  **b.** Is A a candidate key? Prove your answer.
  **c.** Is B a candidate key? Prove your answer.
  **d.** Does B ↠ D? Prove your answer.
  **e.** Does D ↠ B? Prove your answer.

**9.7**  *Given:* R(A, $\underline{B}$, $\underline{C}$, D)

Constraint: The set { R1(A, B), R2(B, C), R3(C, D) } satisfies the lossless join property.

    **a.** Is relation R in projection-join normal form? Explain your answer.

    **b.** Does B → C? Prove your answer.

    **c.** Is AD a candidate key? Prove your answer.

**9.8** *Given:* R($\underline{A}$, B, C, D)

    *Constraints:* A $\twoheadrightarrow$ B

    The set { R1(A, B), R2(B, C) } satisfies the lossless join property.

    **a.** Is relation R in projection-join normal form? Prove your answer.

    **b.** Is relation R in fourth normal form? Prove your answer.

    **c.** Does the set { R1(A, B), R3(A, C) } satisfy the lossless join property? Explain your answer.

**9.9** *Given:* R($\underline{A}$, B, C)

    *Constraint:* The set { R1(A, B), R2(B, C) } satisfies the lossless join property.

    **a.** Does B $\twoheadrightarrow$ C? Prove your answer.

    **b.** Is B a candidate key? Prove your answer.

    **c.** Is relation R in projection-join normal form? Prove your answer.

    **d.** Is relation R in fourth normal form? Prove your answer.

# Chapter 10

# Advanced Normalization Theory

Fourth normal form involves decomposing a relation into two relations by identifying multivalued dependencies. The decomposition can be implemented so that the join of the two relations recreates the original relation exactly (the lossless join property).

A relation in which all multivalued dependencies have been eliminated cannot be decomposed into two relations that satisfy the lossless join property. A database can satisfy the lossless join property, however, although pairs of relations cannot be joined in a lossless manner. A sequence of joins must be developed in which invalid data is created during intermediate joins, but all such invalid data is removed before the join sequence is completed.

Consideration of these complex databases requires additional definitions and theory. The motivation for this theory is that substantial data redundancy may still exist with relations in fourth normal form. A further reduction in data redundancy is possible with fifth normal form.

## 10.1 MUTUAL DEPENDENCY

Consider the following instance of relation R(A, B, C):

| A | B | C |
|---|---|---|
| 1 | 4 | 2 |
| 1 | 5 | 8 |
| 2 | 4 | 8 |

No nontrivial multivalued dependencies exist in this instance. Suppose that R(A, B, C) is decomposed into three relations that yield the following projections:

| R1 | | | R2 | | | R3 | |
|---|---|---|---|---|---|---|---|
| A | B | | A | C | | B | C |
| 1 | 4 | | 1 | 2 | | 4 | 2 |
| 1 | 5 | | 1 | 8 | | 5 | 8 |
| 2 | 4 | | 2 | 8 | | 4 | 8 |

The sequence of joins (R1 x R2) x R3 yields:

| R1 x R2 | | | | R3 | | | (R1 x R2) x R3 | | |
|---|---|---|---|---|---|---|---|---|---|
| A | B | C | | B | C | | A | B | C |
| 1 | 4 | 2 | | 4 | 2 | | 1 | 4 | 2 |
| 1 | 4 | 8 ** | x | 5 | 8 | = | 1 | 4 | 8 ** |
| 1 | 5 | 2 ** | | 4 | 8 | | 1 | 5 | 8 |
| 1 | 5 | 8 | | | | | 2 | 4 | 8 |
| 2 | 4 | 8 | | | | | | | |

The sequence of joins has created the invalid row ( 1 4 8 ). However, suppose that whenever rows ( 1 4 2 ), ( 1 5 8 ) and ( 2 4 8 ) are present in an instance, then row ( 1 4 8 ) must also be present for the instance to be valid. Then the join of R1, R2 and R3 is lossless since row ( 1 4 8 ) is valid. Relation R(A, B, C) is thus decomposed into three relations, with the decomposition satisfying the lossless join property. The data dependency requiring the existence of row ( 1 4 8 ) is called a mutual dependency (or a contextual dependency). Note that, if such a mutual dependency exists, then the original instance of R(A, B, C) is invalid.

The join of the instances of R1 x R2 and R3 removed the invalid row ( 1 5 2 ), which occurs in R1 x R2. In general, for any instance in R(A, B, C), the join of R3 to (R1 x R2) cannot add new rows to the instances of R1 x R2. The join, however, can remove invalid rows. Thus, if R1 x R2 is lossless, then (R1 x R2) x R3 is also lossless.

A mutual dependency between A and B ( A ↔ B ) occurs in R(A, B, C) if the set { R1(A, B), R2(A, C), R3(B, C) } satisfies the lossless join property.

The existence of a mutual dependency can be determined by examining the rows in an instance. For example, consider the following instance of R(A, B, C):

| A | B | C |
|---|---|---|
| 1 | 6 | 3 |
| 1 | 5 | 4 |
| 2 | 6 | 4 |
| 1 | 6 | 4 |

Suppose that two rows exist that contain the same value for A (e.g., the first two rows). Now suppose that another row contains the same value for B as one of the originally considered rows, the same value for C as the other originally considered row and a different value for A from the originally considered rows. The third row in the preceding example satisfies these requirements. Finally, for every occurrence of the situation just described, suppose that a fourth row exists that contains the same value of A as the original two rows and the same values for B and C as the other (third) row. Then $A \leftrightarrow B$. The mutual dependency could also be established by joining the instances of R1(A, B), R2(A, C) and R3(B, C) and verifying that the join is lossless.

If the attributes in a relation are partitioned into sets X, Y and Z:

- If all valid instances contain the same value for X for all rows, then $X \leftrightarrow Y$ trivially.
- If $X \rightarrow Y$, then $X \leftrightarrow Y$.
- If $X \twoheadrightarrow Y$, then $X \leftrightarrow Y$.
- If X is a superkey, then $X \leftrightarrow Y$.

## 10.2 ADDITIONAL ADVANCED DEPENDENCIES

The dependencies discussed in this section were introduced by S. K. Aroura and K. C. Smith ("Graphical Normal Forms Based on Root Dependencies in Relational Data Base Systems," *International Journal of Computer and Information Sciences*, Vol. 10, No. 4, 1981:) Suppose that the attributes comprising a database can be partitioned into $k + 1$ nonempty sets A, Y1, Y2, ... , Yk.

The sets form a **hierarchical dependency** if the $k$ relations R1(A, Y1), R2(A, Y2), ... , Rk(A, Yk) satisfy the lossless join property. The notation A: Y1\Y2\Y3\ ... \Yk is used to represent a hierarchical dependency.

The sets form a **mixed dependency** if relations R1(A, Y1), R2(A, Y2), ... , Rk(A, Yk), Rk+1(Y1, Y2), Rk+2(Y3, Y4), ... , R1/2k(Yk – 1, Yk) satisfy the lossless join property.

The sets form a **codependency** if relations R1(A, Y1), R2(A, Y2), ... , Rk(A, Yk), Rk+1(Y1, Y2), Rk+2(Y2, Y3), Rk+3(Y3, Y4),..., R2k – 1(Yk – 1, Yk) satisfy the lossless join property. The notation A == Y1\Y2\Y3\ ...\Yk is used to represent a codependency.

Multivalued, mutual, hierarchical and mixed dependencies are all special cases of a codependency. Set A is called a **root segment**. The codependency and root segment can be used to model the structure of most data.

## 10.3  FIFTH NORMAL FORM

A relation is in **fifth normal form** if each codependency has a candidate key in the root segment.

Thus the root segment for each codependency must be a superkey. A relation in fifth normal form is also in fourth normal form since a multivalued dependency is also a codependency. For example, suppose that the attributes in a relation can be divided into sets X, Y and Z. Then X ↠ Y implies that relations R1(X, Y) and R2(X, Z) satisfy the lossless join property. Then relations R1(X, Y), R2(X, Z) and R3(Y, Z) also satisfy the lossless join property (which is a codependency). Since the relation is in fifth normal form, X must be a superkey. This is the requirement for fourth normal form.

A relation in fourth normal form is not necessarily in fifth normal form. For example, consider the following instance of the schema R(A, B, C, D), AB ↠ C:

| A | B | C | D |
|---|---|---|---|
| 1 | 1 | 1 | 1 |
| 1 | 2 | 1 | 2 |
| 2 | 1 | 1 | 2 |
| 2 | 2 | 2 | 2 |

This instance satisfies fourth normal form since AB contains no duplicate values. However, consider the following set of relations, which satisfies the lossless join property: R1(A, B), R2(A, C), R3(A, D), R4(B, C) and R5(C, D). This is a codependency with A as the root segment. The instance does not satisfy fifth normal form, however, since the instance contains duplicate values in A.

## 10.4 SUMMARY OF NORMAL FORMS

Consider relation R(X, Y, Z). If $X \rightarrow Y$, then $X \twoheadrightarrow Y$ and if $X \twoheadrightarrow Y$, then $X \leftrightarrow Y$. If $X \twoheadrightarrow Y$, however, this does not imply that $X \rightarrow Y$. Also, if $X \leftrightarrow Y$, this does not imply that $X \twoheadrightarrow Y$. The following table summarizes the possibilities:

| $X \rightarrow Y$ | $X \twoheadrightarrow Y$ | $X \leftrightarrow Y$ |
|---|---|---|
| true | true | true |
| false | true | true |
| false | false | true |
| false | false | false |

Suppose that X is not a superkey. A relation is not in Boyce-Codd, fourth or fifth normal forms if a "true" appears in the first column. A relation is not in fourth or fifth normal form if a "true" appears in the second column. A relation is not in fifth normal form if a "true" appears in the third column.

Relations not in Boyce-Codd or fourth normal form should be decomposed into two or more relations that satisfy the lossless join property. At least two relations are required since $X \rightarrow Y$ or $X \twoheadrightarrow Y$ means that R1(X, Y) x R2(X, Z) is lossless.

Relations in fourth normal form but not in fifth normal form should be decomposed into three or more relations that satisfy the lossless join property. At least three relations are required since $X \leftrightarrow Y$ means that R1(X, Y) x R2(X, Z) x R3(Y, Z) is lossless.

Conversely, suppose that X is a superkey for every functional dependency $X \rightarrow Y$. Then the relation is in Boyce-Codd normal form. The relation is in fourth normal form if X is a superkey for every multivalued dependency $X \twoheadrightarrow Y$. Note that set Z is required in the preceding relation since $X \twoheadrightarrow Y$ is trivially true if Z is not included.

## Summary

The dependency structure among attributes can be expanded further by considering mutual dependencies, hierarchical dependencies, mixed dependencies and codependencies. Consideration of these advanced dependencies leads to the definition of fifth normal form.

## Exercises

10.1 Given relational schema R(A, B, C), A ↔ B:
   a. Is the join of the projections of R1(A, B) and R2(A, C) lossless? Explain your answer.
   b. Is the join of the projections of R1(A, B) and R3(B, C) lossless? Explain your answer.
   c. Is the join of the projections of R2(A, C) and R3(B, C) lossless? Explain your answer.
   d. Is the join of the projections of R1(A, B), R2(A, C) and R3(B, C) lossless? Explain your answer.
   e. Does B ↔ A? Explain your answer.
   f. Does C ↔ A? Explain your answer.

10.2 Given R(A, B, C), determine which of the following instances satisfies A ↔ B:

| a. A | B | C | b. A | B | C | c. A | B | C | d. A | B | C | e. A | B | C |
|---|---|---|---|---|---|---|---|---|---|---|---|---|---|---|
| 1 | 2 | 1 | 1 | 1 | 1 | 1 | 1 | 1 | 1 | 2 | 1 | 1 | 1 | 1 |
| 1 | 1 | 2 | 1 | 2 | 2 | 1 | 2 | 2 | 1 | 1 | 2 | 2 | 1 | 1 |
| 1 | 2 | 2 | 2 | 2 | 1 | 1 | 2 | 1 | | | | 1 | 2 | 2 |
| 2 | 2 | 2 | 1 | 1 | 2 | 2 | 1 | 2 | | | | 2 | 2 | 2 |
| | | | | | | 2 | 2 | 1 | | | | 1 | 1 | 2 |
| | | | | | | | | | | | | 2 | 1 | 2 |

10.3 Given relational schema R(A, B, C), A ↔ B:
   a. What rows must be included with ( 1 1 1 ), ( 1 2 2 ) and ( 2 1 2 ) to create a valid instance?
   b. What rows must be included with ( 1 1 1 ) and ( 1 1 2 ) to create a valid instance?
   c. What rows must be included with ( 1 1 1 ), ( 1 2 2 ), ( 2 1 2 ) and ( 2 2 1 ) to create a valid instance?
   d. What rows must be included with ( 1 1 2 ), ( 2 2 2 ) and ( 3 2 1 ) to create a valid instance?

**10.4** Given relational schema R(A, B, C), A → B:

    **a.** Does A ↔ B? Prove your answer.

    **b.** Does C ↔ B? Prove your answer.

    **c.** Does C ↠ B? Prove your answer.

**10.5** Given relational schema R(A, B, C), A ↠ B:

    **a.** Does A ↔ B? Prove your answer.

    **b.** Does A → B? Prove your answer.

    **c.** Does A ↠ C? Prove your answer.

**10.6** Given relational schema R(A, B, C), A ↔ B:

    **a.** Does A → B? Prove your answer.

    **b.** Does A ↠ B? Prove your answer.

    **c.** Does A ↠ C? Prove your answer.

    **d.** Does A ↠ BC? Prove your answer.

**10.7** Given the following instance of R(A, B, C):

| A | B | C |
|---|---|---|
| 1 | 1 | 1 |
| 1 | 2 | 2 |
| 2 | 1 | 2 |
| 2 | 2 | 1 |

Find the join of the projections of this instance on R1(A, B), R2(A, C) and R3(B, C). Does this instance satisfy A ↔ B?

**10.8** Given relational schema R(A, B, C, D), A → B and A → D:

    **a.** Does A: B\C\D? Explain your answer.

    **b.** Does A ↔ B? Explain your answer.

    **c.** Does A ↔ CD? Explain your answer.

    **d.** Does C: A\B\D? Explain your answer.

**10.9** Given relational schema R(A, B, C, D), A → B:

    **a.** Does A: B\C\D? Explain your answer.

    **b.** Does CD ↔ A? Explain your answer.

    **c.** Does B: A\C\D? Explain your answer.

    **d.** Does B ↔ CD? Explain your answer.

**10.10** Given relational schema R(A, B, C, D), A ↠ B:

    **a.** Does A: B\C\D? Explain your answer.

    **b.** Does C ↔ D? Explain your answer.

    **c.** Does A ↔ CD? Explain your answer.

**10.11** Given R(A, B, C):

    **a.** Explain why A ↠ B and A: B\C are equivalent constraints.

    b. Are A → B and A: B\C equivalent constraints? Explain your answer.

    c. Given A: B\C, does A ↔ B? Explain your answer.

    d. Given A ↔ B, does A: B\C? Explain your answer.

10.12 Given relational schema R(A, B, C, D), A: B\C\D:

    a. What rows must be included with ( 1 1 1 1 ) and ( 1 2 2 2 ) to create a valid instance?

    b. What rows must be included with ( 1 1 1 1 ) and ( 1 1 1 2 ) to create a valid instance?

    c. What rows must be included with ( 1 1 1 1 ) and ( 1 1 2 2 ) to create a valid instance?

10.13 Given relational schema R(A, B, C, D, E, F, G, H), A: B\C\D\E\F\G\H, and the following instance:

| A | B | C | D | E | F | G | H |
|---|---|---|---|---|---|---|---|
| 1 | 1 | 1 | 1 | 1 | 1 | 1 | 1 |
| 1 | 2 | 2 | 2 | 2 | 2 | 2 | 2 |

How many rows must be added to create a valid instance?

10.14 Given R(A, B, C, D), determine whether each of the following statements is true or false. If the statement is false, give an instance that illustrates why it is.

    a. If A → B and A → C, then A == B\C\D.

    b. If C → D, then A == B\C\D.

    c. If C ↠ D, then A == B\C\D.

    d. If B → D, then A == B\C\D.

    e. If B ↠ D, then A == B\C\D.

    f. If A ↔ B, then A == B\C\D.

    g. If A → B and A → D, then A == B\C\D.

    h. If A → B and A ↠ D/B, then A == B\C\D.

    i. If A → B and A ↠ D, then A == B\C\D.

10.15 Given relational schema R(A, B, C, D), A == B\C\D:

    a. Consider the instance

| A | B | C | D |
|---|---|---|---|
| 1 | 1 | 1 | 1 |
| 1 | 2 | 2 | 2 |

What rows must also be included to create a valid instance?

b. Consider the instance

| A | B | C | D |
|---|---|---|---|
| 1 | 1 | 1 | 1 |
| 1 | 2 | 1 | 2 |

What rows must also be included to create a valid instance?

c. Consider the instance

| A | B | C | D |
|---|---|---|---|
| 1 | 1 | 1 | 1 |
| 2 | 2 | 1 | 2 |

What rows must also be included to create a valid instance?

10.16 Given R(A, B, C), explain why A ↔ B and A == B\C are equivalent constraints.

10.17 Given R(A, B, C, D), explain why A: B\C\D and A == B\C\D are not equivalent constraints.

# Appendix

# A Mathematical Representation of Dependencies and Normal Forms

In this Appendix data normalization is approached from a mathematical perspective. Mathematical representations of functional and multivalued dependencies, normal forms, the lossless join property and candidate keys are presented. The necessary and sufficient conditions for the lossless join property are proven. An algorithm to determine whether a relation is in Boyce-Codd normal form is given as is the mathematical proof that fourth normal form implies Boyce-Codd normal form.

The mathematical presentation is based in part on the work of T. T. Lee ("An Algebraic Theory of Relational Databases," *Bell Systems Journal*, Vol. 62, No. 10, December 1983). One application of this theory is the development of a computer program that translates functional dependencies into relational database designs satisfying the lossless join property, with each relation in Boyce-Codd normal form.

## A.1 CANDIDATE KEYS AND FUNCTIONAL DEPENDENCIES

The mathematical representation of normalization theory begins by defining a function that maps pairs of rows in a relational schema instance onto the set $\{0, 1\}$. Pairs that contain identical values in a given set of attributes are mapped to 1. Pairs that are not identical are mapped to 0.

A **relational schema** is a set of attributes $A_j$, $R = \{A_1, A_2, \dots, A_n\}$ and a set of data constraints (e.g., functional and multivalued dependencies).

An **instance** $r$ of a relational schema is a set of rows $(a_{i,1}, a_{i,2}, \dots, a_{i,n})$ containing data elements $a_{i,j}$ that populate relation R.

An instance is **valid** if the data elements satisfy the set of constraints of the relational schema.

Let

>XY denote the union of X and Y
>$X \cap Y$ denote the intersection of X and Y
>$X - Y$ denote the difference of X and Y
>$\lesssim$ denote not $\leq$

For any instance $r$, let

$$g_{i,j}(A_k) \begin{cases} = 1 \text{ if } a_{i,k} \text{ and } a_{j,k} \text{ are identical} \\ \\ = 0 \text{ if } a_{i,k} \text{ and } a_{j,k} \text{ are not identical} \end{cases}$$

$$g_{i,j}(X) = \min_{(k \text{ in } x)} \{g_{i,j}(A_k)\} \text{ where } X \text{ is a subset of } R.$$

$$G(X) = \text{vector } (g_{i,j}(X)) \text{ for all pairs } (i,j) \text{ in } r, i < j.$$

Thus $G(X)$ is a vector of zero and one values that indicate which pairs of rows in r contain duplicate values in X. $G(R) = 0$ (where 0 is the null vector) for all $r$ since no duplicate rows are permitted in the entire relational set $R$. Let $X$, $Y$, $U$ and $V$ represent subsets of $R$. Then, for any $r$, define:

$G(X) \leq G(Y)$ if $g_{i,j}(X) \leq g_{i,j}(Y)$ for all $(i, j)$
$G(X) \lesssim G(Y)$ if $g_{i,j}(X) > g_{i,j}(Y)$ for some $(i, j)$
$G(X) < G(Y)$ if $G(X) \leq G(Y)$ and $g_{i,j}(X) < g_{i,j}(Y)$ for some $(i, j)$
$G(X) \cdot G(Y)$ is the vector with elements $g_{i,j}(X) \cdot g_{i,j}(Y)$.

Now

$G(Y) \leq G(X)$ if $X$ is a subset of $Y$ since $\min_{(k \text{ in } Y)}\{g_{i,j}(A_k)\} \leq \min_{(k \text{ in } X)}\{g_{i,j}(A_k)\}$

$G(XY) = G(X) \cdot G(Y)$ since $\min_{(k \text{ in } XY)}\{g_{i,j}(A_k)\} = \min_{(k \text{ in } X)}\{g_{i,j}(A_k)\} \cdot \min_{(k \text{ in } Y)}\{g_{i,j}(A_k)\}$

$G(X) \leq G(X \cap Y)$ since $X \cap Y$ is a subset of $X$
$G^2(X) = G(X)$ since $g^2_{i,j}(A_k) = g_{i,j}(A_k)$

If $G(X) \leq G(U)$ and $G(Y) \leq G(V)$, then $G(XY) \leq G(UV)$. This follows since if $g_{i,j}(X) = 1$ and $g_{i,j}(Y) = 1$, then $g_{i,j}(U) = g_{i,j}(V) = 1$.

If $0 < G(X) \leq G(Y)$, then $0 < G(XY)$. This follows since there must exist a pair $(i, j)$ such that $g_{i,j}(X) = g_{i,j}(Y) = 1$ and $G(XY) = G(X) \cdot G(Y)$.

## A.2 REPRESENTATION OF FUNCTIONAL DEPENDENCIES

Dependency $X \to Y$ implies that duplicate rows in $X$ are also duplicate in $Y$. Thus $X \to Y$ if and only if $G(X) \leq G(Y)$ for all valid instances $r$.

A **superkey** of a relational schema is any subset $K$ of $R$ such that $G(K) = 0$ for all valid $r$.

$K$ is a **candidate key** if $K$ has minimum cardinality among all superkeys. Any candidate key can be selected as the primary key.

For example, consider the relational schema $R(A, B, C)$, $A \to B$ and $A \to C$. Given these dependencies, $G(A) \leq G(B)$ and $G(A) \leq G(C)$ for all valid $r$. Therefore $G(A) \leq G(BC)$ and thus $G(A) \leq G(A) \cdot G(BC) = G(R)$ (since $G(R) = 0$, and $G(A) \leq G(R)$, $G(A) = 0$ for all valid $r$).

Thus $A$ is a superkey. $A$ is also a candidate key since no superkey can have cardinality less than 1. No other candidate key is implied by the set of constraints.

## A.3 FIRST, SECOND AND THIRD NORMAL FORMS

**First normal form** requires that no repeating groups are contained within the relation.

The mathematical representations in this chapter assume that the relations are in first normal form with K as the primary key.

A relation is in **second normal form** if the following conditions are satisfied in some valid instance: For each proper subset Y of $K$, $G(Y) \stackrel{\sim}{\leq} G(A_k)$ for all $A_k$ in $(R - K)$.

A relation is in **third normal form** if whenever $G(X) \leq G(A_k)$ in all valid instances, then either

$$G(X) = 0$$

or

$$A_k \text{ belongs to } X$$

or

$$A_k \text{ belongs to some candidate key}$$

## A.4 BOYCE-CODD NORMAL FORM

A relation is in **Boyce-Codd normal form** if whenever $G(X) \leq G(Y)$ holds in all valid $r$, then either

$$G(X) = 0$$

or

$$Y \text{ is a subset of } X$$

For example, consider the relational schema $R(A, B, C, D)$, $AB \to C$ and $AB \to D$. Then $G(AB) = 0$ for all valid $r$ and $K = AB$. A valid instance need satisfy only $G(AB) \leq G(C)$ and $G(AB) \leq G(D)$. Consider the instance:

| A | B | C | D |
|---|---|---|---|
| 1 | 1 | 1 | 1 |
| 1 | 2 | 2 | 1 |
| 2 | 1 | 2 | 1 |
| 2 | 2 | 2 | 2 |
| 1 | 3 | 1 | 1 |
| 3 | 1 | 1 | 1 |

This is a valid instance and the following are true:

$$G(A) \lesseqgtr G(C)$$
$$G(A) \lesseqgtr G(D)$$
$$G(B) \lesseqgtr G(C)$$
$$G(B) \lesseqgtr G(D)$$

The relation is thus in second normal form. The relation is also in third normal form since neither $G(C) \leq G(D)$ nor $G(D) \leq G(C)$ are satisfied in the instance. In addition, the relation is in Boyce-Codd normal form since whenever $G(X) \leq G(Y)$ in all valid instances, then either AB is a subset of X or Y is a subset of X.

An algorithm exists to determine whether a relation is in Boyce-Codd normal form. The procedure involves computing a set of attributes for each functional dependency in the schema. The relation is in Boyce-Codd normal form if and only if the computed set is equal to R for each dependency.

Let $X_i \rightarrow Y_i$, $i = i, \dots, m$ denote the $i^{th}$ dependency in the schema and $S_i$ denote the computed set of attributes. The algorithm for determining $S_i$ is as follows:

1. $S_i = X_i Y_i$
2. For each $j = 1, 2, \dots, m$ ($j \neq i$), if $X_j$ is a subset of $S_i$, then add $Y_j$ to $S_i$.
3. Stop if $S_i = R$.
4. If $S_i \neq R$ and at least one new attribute was added to $S_i$ in step 2, then go to step 2.
5. Stop if $S_i \neq R$ and no new attributes were added in step 2. In this case, the relation is not in Boyce-Codd normal form.

All nontrivial functional dependencies must be used in this algorithm. Therefore any nontrivial dependencies implied by the set of constraints must be included.

The relational schema discussed previously in this section will be used to illustrate the algorithm. No nontrivial functional dependencies are implied by the constraints. The algorithm proceeds as follows:

For constraint $AB \rightarrow C$:

1. $S_1 = ABC$
2. $S_1 = S_1 C = ABCD$ since AB is a subset of $S_1$.
3. Stop since $S_1 = R$.

For constraint $AB \rightarrow D$:

1. $S_2 = ABD$
2. $S_2 = S_2 C = ABCD$ since AB is a subset of $S_2$.
3. Stop since $S_2 = R$.

The relation is in Boyce-Codd normal form since $S_1 = S_2 = R$.

## A.5  MULTIVALUED DEPENDENCY

The multivalued dependency $X \twoheadrightarrow Y$ implies that whenever a pair of rows in an instance are identical in $X$, then the two rows created by interchanging the $Y$ values in the pair are also in the instance.

**Multivalued dependencies** are formally defined as follows: $X \twoheadrightarrow Y$ if and only if the following conditions hold for all valid instances $r$: If $g_{i,j}(X) = 1$ for some pair $(i,j)$ in $r$, then there exist rows $k_1, k_2$ in $r$ such that:

1. $g_{ik1}(Y) = 1 \, g_{jk1}(R - Y) = 1$
2. $g_{jk2}(Y) = 1 \, g_{ik2}(R - Y) = 1$

If $Y$ is a subset of $X$, then $X \twoheadrightarrow Y$ is trivially true since conditions 1 and 2 are satisfied by taking $k_1 = j$ and $k_2 = i$. If $XY = R$, then $R - Y$ is a subset of $X$. Therefore, if $XY = R$, then $X \twoheadrightarrow Y$ is trivially true since conditions 1 and 2 are satisfied by $k_1 = j$ and $k_2 = i$.

## A.6 FOURTH NORMAL FORM

A relation is in **fourth normal form** if whenever $g_{i,j}(X) = 1$ implies conditions 1 and 2 (stated in the previous section) for all valid instances, then either:

$$G(X) = 0$$

or

The multivalued dependency is trivial.

If $X \to Y$, then $X \twoheadrightarrow Y$ since whenever $g_{i,j}(X) = 1$, then $g_{i,j}(Y) = 1$ and conditions 1 and 2 are satisfied by $k_1 = j$ and $k_2 = i$.

A relation in fourth normal form is also in Boyce-Codd normal form. Suppose that the relation is in fourth normal form but not in Boyce-Codd normal form. Then there exist subsets $X$ and $Y$ of $R$ with $Y$ not a subset of $X$ such that $X \to Y$ but $G(X) > 0$ for some valid $r$. However, $X \twoheadrightarrow Y$ since $X \to Y$ and since the relation is in fourth normal form, either:

$$G(X) = 0 \text{ for all valid } r$$

or

$$X \twoheadrightarrow Y \text{ is trivial.}$$

$G(X) > 0$ for some valid $r$, however, and thus $X \twoheadrightarrow Y$ must be trivial. $Y$ is not a subset of $X$, and thus $XY$ must equal $R$. Therefore there is a valid $r$ such that $0 < G(X) \leq G(Y)$. Thus $G(R) > 0$ is a contradiction.

A relation not in fourth normal form can be decomposed into two relations that satisfy the lossless join property. The nontrivial multivalued dependency $X \twoheadrightarrow Y$, for which $G(X) > 0$ for some $r$, is used to determine the decomposition. The necessary and sufficient conditions for a lossless join are given in the following theorem.

**Theorem:** Let $R = R_1 R_2$ and $V = R_1 \cap R_2$ be nonempty. The relations $R_1$ and $R_2$ satisfy the **lossless join property** if and only if $V \twoheadrightarrow (R_1 - V)$ or $V \twoheadrightarrow (R_2 - V)$.

*Proof:* Let $r$ be any valid instance of the relational schema for $R$ and let $r_1$ and $r_2$ be the projections of $r$ on $R_1$ and $R_2$, respectively. Let $i$ and $j$ be rows in $r$ such that $g_{i,j}(V) = 1$. Let $i_1$ and $i_2$ be the projections of $i$ on $R_1$ and $R_2$, respectively. Let $j_1$ and $j_2$ be the projections of $j$ on $R_1$ and $R_2$, respectively. Then:

- Assume that $V \twoheadrightarrow (R_1 - V)$. The join of $r_1$ and $r_2$ is lossless if the join of $i_1$ and $j_2$ is in $r$ and the join of $j_1$ and $i_2$ is in $r$. Since $V \twoheadrightarrow (R_1 - V)$, there exist $k_1$ and $k_2$ in $r$ such that:

$$g_{i,k_1}(R_1 - V) = 1 \qquad\qquad g_{j,k_1}(R - (R_1 - V)) = 1$$

  and

$$g_{j,k_2}(R_1 - V) = 1 \qquad\qquad g_{i,k_2}(R - (R_1 - V)) = 1$$

  Since $R_2 = R - (R_1 - V)$, $k_1$ is the join of $i_1$ and $j_2$ and $k_2$ is the join of $j_1$ and $i_2$. A similar proof holds if $V \twoheadrightarrow (R_2 - V)$.
- Assume that $R_1$ and $R_2$ satisfy the lossless join property. Let $k_1$ be the join of $i_1$ and $j_2$ and $k_2$ be the join of $j_1$ and $i_2$. Then $g_{i,j}(V) = 1$ and $g_{i1,k_1}(R_1 - V) = 1$, $g_{j,k_1}(V) = 1$, $g_{j2,k_1}(R_2 - V) = 1$ and $g_{j1,k_2}(R_1 - V) = 1$, $g_{i,k_2}(V) = 1$, $g_{i2,k_2}(R_2 - V) = 1$. Since $g_{i,j,i}(R_1 - V) = 1$, $g_{i,j2}(R_2 - V) = 1$ and $g_{j,j1}(R_1 - V) = 1$, $g_{i,j2}(R_2 - V) = 1$, then $g_{i,k_1}(R_1 - V) = 1$, $g_{j,k_1}(V) = 1$, $g_{j,k_1}(R_2 - V) = 1$ and $g_{j,k_2}(R_1 - V) = 1$, $g_{i,k_2}(V) = 1$, $g_{i,k_2}(R_2 - V) = 1$. Since $R_1$ and $R_2$ satisfy the lossless join property,

then $k_1$ and $k_2$ are in $r$. However, $R - (R_1 - V) = V(R_2 - V)$, so $g_{jk1}(R - (R_1 - V)) = 1$ and $g_{jk2}(R - (R - V)) = 1$ and thus $V \twoheadrightarrow (R_1 - V)$. Also, $V \twoheadrightarrow (R_2 - V)$ since $R - (R_2 - V) = V(R_1 - V)$ and $g_{i,j}(V) = 1$.

## Summary

Data normalization can be approached from a rigorous, mathematical perspective, and readers with a mathematical background may gain additional insights into the data normalization process. Dependency structures, candidate keys, the lossless join property and normal forms can all be defined in mathematical notation. The rigorous definitions are also useful in developing computer programs to implement data normalization theory.

## Exercises

A.1   Given $R(A, B, C, D)$ and $G(AB) \leq G(C)$ for all valid instances, determine which of the following are true. Explain each answer.

a. $AB \rightarrow C$
b. $AB \rightarrow D$
c. $AB \twoheadrightarrow C$
d. $AB \twoheadrightarrow D$
e. $C \rightarrow A$

A.2   Given $R(A, B, C)$ and $G(AB) \leq G(C)$ for all valid instances:

a. Prove that $AB$ is a superkey.
b. Give a valid instance to show that $AC$ is not a superkey.

A.3   Given $R(A, B, C, D)$, $X = ABC$, $Y = A$ and $Z = CD$, determine which of the following statements are true for all valid instances. Explain each answer.

a. $G(X) \leq G(Y)$
b. $G(Y) \leq G(X)$
c. $G(X) \cdot G(Z) = 0$
d. $G(X) \cdot G(Y) = 0$
e. $G(X) \leq G(X \cap Z)$
f. $G(X \cap Z) \leq G(X)$
g. $G(Z) \cdot G(Z) = G(Z)$

A.4  Prove that if $X \to Y$ then $XZ \to Y$.

A.5  Prove that if $X \to Y$ and $Y \to Z$, then $X \to Z$.

A.6  Given $R(A, B, C, D)$, $AB \to C$ and $G(AB) > 0$ for all valid $r$:
   a. Prove that $G(C) > 0$ for all valid $r$.
   b. Prove that $G(ABC) > 0$ for all valid $r$.
   c. Prove that $G(AB) \cdot G(D) = 0$ for all valid $r$.

A.7  Let $X$, $Y$ and $Z$ be subsets of a relation $R$. Prove that if $X \to Y$ and $X \to Z$, then $X \to YZ$.

A.8  Given $R(\underline{A}, \underline{B}, C, D)$, $A \to C$, prove that this relation is not in second normal form.

A.9  Given $R(\underline{A}, B, C)$, $G(B) \le G(C)$ and $G(B) \le G(A)$ for all valid instances, show that this relation is in third normal form.

A.10 Given $R(\underline{A}, B, C)$, $G(B) \le G(C)$ for all valid instances, give a valid instance to show that this relation is not in third normal form.

A.11 Given $R(A, B, C)$, $A \to B$, $A \to C$ and $B \to C$, use the algorithm presented in this Appendix to show that this relation is not in Boyce-Codd normal form.

A.12 Given $R(A, B, C, D)$, $AB \to C$, $C \to D$, $D \to A$ and $D \to B$, use the algorithm presented in this Appendix to determine whether this relation is in Boyce-Codd normal form.

A.13 Given $R(A, B, C)$ and $A \twoheadrightarrow B$. Suppose that $g_{i,j}(A) = 1$ in some valid $r$. What other rows must also be included in $r$?

A.14 Given $R(A, B, C, D)$ and $AB \twoheadrightarrow C$, what other rows must be included so that the following instance is valid?

| A | B | C | D |
|---|---|---|---|
| 1 | 1 | 1 | 2 |
| 1 | 1 | 2 | 1 |

A.15 Given $R(A, B, C)$ and $A \twoheadrightarrow B$, prove that $A \twoheadrightarrow C$.

A.16 Given $R(A, B, C, D)$ and $AB \twoheadrightarrow C$, give a valid instance with four rows to show that this relation is not in fourth normal form.

A.17 Given $R(A, B, C)$ and $AB \twoheadrightarrow C$, prove that this relation is in fourth normal form.

A.18 Give necessary and sufficient conditions so that relations $R1(A, B, C)$ and $R2(B, C, D)$ satisfy the lossless join property.

A.19 Consider $R(A, B, C, D)$, $R1(A, C, D)$ and $R2(B, C)$. If $R1$ and $R2$ satisfy the lossless join property, then what dependencies are included in the relational schema for $R$?

A.20 Given $R(A, B, C)$ and $A \to B$, prove that $A \twoheadrightarrow C$

# Glossary of Terms

| | |
|---|---|
| Attribute | A field in a record (a column in a relation). |
| Boyce-Codd normal form | A relation in first normal form with the property that whenever $X \rightarrow A$ and A does not belong to X, then X is a superkey. |
| Candidate key | An attribute (or combination of attributes) with minimum cardinality that uniquely identifies a row. |
| Composite key | A key that contains more than one attribute. |
| Constraint | Any limitation placed on a relation. |
| Decomposition of relation R | A set of relations $R_i$ such that the union of the set is relation R. |
| Dependency preservation | A decomposition in which all the original functional dependencies can be implied from the functional dependencies in the relations forming the decomposition. |
| Determinant group | The set of attributes X in the functional dependency $X \rightarrow A$. |
| Domain | The set of possible values that an attribute can assume. |
| Domain-key normal form | A relation in which all constraints are implied by the set of key dependencies and the domains of the attributes. |
| Fifth normal form | A relation in which each codependency has a candidate key in the root segment. |
| First normal form | A relation that contains no repeating groups. |
| Foreign key | An attribute that appears as a nonkey attribute in one relation and as a primary key attribute (or part of a primary key) in another relation. |

| | |
|---|---|
| Fourth normal form | A relation in which the implying set of each multivalued dependency is a superkey. |
| Fully functionally dependent | An attribute (or group of attributes) X is fully functionally dependent on another collection of attributes Y, if X is functionally dependent on the whole of Y but not on any subset of Y. |
| Functional dependence | Attribute A is functionally dependent on set X, if at every instant in time, each value of X has no more than one value of A associated with it in the relation (i.e., X identifies A). |
| Instance | A set of one or more rows that populates a relation. |
| Join | A relational operator used to combine data from two relations. |
| Join dependency | See Projection-join dependency. |
| Key dependency | A constraint that requires a set of attributes to be a superkey. |
| Logical database | A database as perceived by its users; the logical database may be structured differently from the physical database. |
| Lossless join | A set of relations has a lossless join if the instances of the relations can be joined without creating invalid rows. |
| Multivalued dependency | Y is multivalued dependent on X if, whenever an instance contains duplicate rows in X, the Y values in the rows can be interchanged creating two rows that are also in the instance. |
| Mutual dependency | A and B form a mutual dependency in the relation R(A, B, C) if the set { R1(A,B), R2(A,C), R3(B,C) } satisfies the lossless join property. |
| Normalization | The decomposition of complex data structures into relations. |
| Primary key | A candidate key that is selected as the unique identifier. |

| | |
|---|---|
| Project | A relational operator used to create a new relation from a subset of another relation. |
| Projection-join dependency | A constraint that requires that a set of relations satisfy the lossless join property. |
| Projection-join normal form | A relation in which the set of key dependencies guarantees that the set of projection-join dependencies is satisfied. |
| Relation | A two-dimensional data structure, usually conceived as a table, in which the columns are attributes and the rows are instances. |
| Repeating group | A sequence of logically related attributes that may occur multiple times within row occurrences. |
| Schema | A set of attributes, dependencies and other constraints that characterize a relation. |
| Second normal form | A relation in first normal form in which every nonkey attribute is fully functionally dependent on the primary key. |
| Semantic disintegrity | Undesirable results that can occur with the use of relational database query languages. |
| Subkey | A subset of the set of attributes that collectively define a primary key. |
| Superkey | Any set of attributes for which no duplicate rows exist in any valid instance of the relation. |
| Third normal form | A relation in second normal form in which no transitive dependencies exist. |
| Transitive dependence | Attribute C is transitively dependent on attribute A if attribute B exists such that A $\rightarrow$ B, B $\rightarrow$ C and B $\nrightarrow$ A (essentially an undesirable dependency between nonkey attributes). |
| Tuple | A row in an instance. |
| Valid instance | An instance in which all the dependencies and other constraints specified in the schema are satisfied. |

# Glossary of Symbols

| | |
|---|---|
| $X \rightarrow Y$ | Y is functionally dependent on X. |
| $X \nrightarrow Y$ | Y is not functionally dependent on X. |
| AB | The union of relations A and B. |
| $A \cap B$ | The intersection of relations A and B. |
| $A - B$ | The difference of relations A and B. |
| $X \twoheadrightarrow Y$ | Y is multivalued dependent on X. |
| $X \twoheadrightarrow Y/V$ | Y is multivalued dependent on X in the context of V. |
| $A \times B$ | The join of relations A and B. |
| $A \leftrightarrow B$ | Relations A and B are mutually dependent. |
| A: Y1\Y2\Y3\ ... \Yk | A hierarchical dependency among A, Y1, Y2, Y3, ... , Yk. |
| A == Y1\Y2\Y3\ ... \Yk | A codependency among A, Y1, Y2, Y3, ... , Yk. |

# Bibliography

The Bibliography is divided into two parts. The first part lists the references in which major topics were originally defined or introduced. The second contains other references that expand, clarify or otherwise help teach the theory of data normalization.

## Part I: Original References

First, second and third normal forms
Codd, E. F., "Further Normalization of the Data Base Relational Model," *Data Base Systems,* Courant Computer Science Symposia Series, Vol. 6, Prentice-Hall, Englewood Cliffs, N.J. (1972)

Boyce-Codd normal form
Heath, I. J., "Unacceptable File Operations in a Relational Data Base," *Proceedings, 1971 ACM SIGFIDET Workshop on Data Description, Access and Control* (November 1971)

Codd, E. F., "Recent Investigations into Relational Data Base Systems," *Proceedings, IFIP Congress,* New York (1974)

Fourth normal form
Fagin, R., "Multivalued Dependencies and a New Normal Form For Relational Databases," *ACM Transactions on Database Systems,* Vol. 2, No. 3 (September 1977)

Projection-Join normal form
Fagin, R., "Normal Forms and Relational Database Operators," *Proceedings, 1979 ACM SIGMOD International Conference on Management of Data,* Boston

Domain-key normal form
Fagin, R. "A Normal Form for Relational Databases that Is Based on Domains and Keys," *ACM Transactions on Database Systems,* Vol. 6, No. 3 (September 1981); also in *IBM Research Report,* RJ 2520 (32950), (1978)

Functional dependencies and inference axioms

Armstrong, W.W., "Dependency Structures of Database Relationships," *Proceedings, IFIP Congress*, North Holland, New York (1974)

Multivalued dependency inference axioms

Beeri, C., Fagin, R., and Howard, J. H., "A Complete Axiomatization for Functional and Multivalued Dependencies in Database Relations," *Proceedings, 1977 ACM SIGMOD International Conference on Management of Data*, Toronto (August 1977)

Mutual dependencies

Nicolas, J. M., "Mutual Dependencies and Some Results on Undecomposable Relations," *Proceedings, Fourth International Conference on Very Large Data Bases* Berlin (1978)

Decomposition into third normal form with lossless join is achievable

Heath, I. J., "Unacceptable File Operations in a Relational Database," *Proceedings, 1971 ACM SIGFIDET Workshop on Data Description, Access and Control* (November 1971)

Decomposition into fourth normal form with lossless joins is achievable

Fagin, R., "Multivalued Dependencies and a New Normal Form for Relational Databases," *ACM Transactions on Database Systems* Vol. 2, No. 3 (September 1977)

Decomposition into fifth normal form with lossless joins is not always achievable with a decomposition into two relations

Aho, A. V., Beeri, C. and Ullman, J. D., "The Theory of Joins in Relational Databases," *ACM Transactions on Database Systems*, Vol. 4, No. 3 (September 1979), first published in *Proceedings, 19th IEEE Symposium on Foundations of Computer Science* (October 1977)

Decomposition into projection-join normal form with lossless joins is achievable

Fagin, R., "Normal Forms and Relational Database Operators," *Proceedings, 1979 ACM SIGMOD International Conference on Management of Data*, Boston


Part II: Other References

Aho, A. V., Hopcropft, J. E., and Ullman, J. D., *The Design and Analysis of Computer Algorithms*, Addison-Wesley, Reading, Mass. (1974)

Arora, A. K., and Carlson, C. R., "The Information Preserving Properties of Relational Database Transformations," *Proceedings of the Fourth International Conference on Very Large Data Bases*, West Berlin (September 1978)

Arora, S. K., and Smith, K. C., "Graphical Normal Forms Based on Root Dependencies in Relational Data Base Systems," *International Journal of Computer and Information Sciences*, Vol. 10, No. 4 (1981)

Arora, S. K., and Smith, K. C., "A Normal Form Based on Theta-Join and Projection for Relational Data Bases," *IEEE COMPCON FALL*, Washington, D.C., (1980)

Arora, S.K., and Smith, K.C., "A Theory of Well Connected Relations," *Journal of Information Sciences*, Vol. 19 (1979)

Arora, S. K., and Smith, K. C., "A Dependency Theory and a "New" Dependency for Relational Data Bases," *ACM Computer Science Conference* (1979)

Arora, S. K., and Smith, K. C., "Well Connected Relations in Dependency Structures of Data Bases," *Conference of the Canadian Information Processing Society*, Quebec City (1979)

Beeri, C., "On the Membership Problem for Functional and Multivalued Dependencies in Relational Databases," *ACM Transactions on Database Systems*, Vol. 5, No. 3 (September 1980)

Beeri, C., and Bernstein, P. A., "Computational Problems Related to the Design of Normal Form Relational Schemes," *ACM Transactions on Database Systems*, Vol. 4, No. 1 (March 1979)

Beeri, C., Bernstein, P. A., and Goodman, N. A., "A Sophisticate's Introduction to Database Normalization Theory," *Proceedings of the 4th International Conference on Very Large Data Bases*, West Berlin (September 1978)

Beeri, C., Fagin, R., Maier, D., and Yannakakis, M., "On the Desirability of Acyclic Database Schemes," *Journal of the ACM*, Vol. 30, No. 3 (July 1983)

Beeri, C., and Kifer, M., "Elimination of Intersection Anomalies from Database Schemes," *Journal of the ACM*, Vol. 33, No. 3 (July 1986)

Beeri, C., and Kifer, M., "An Integrated Approach to Logical Design of Relational Database Schemes," *ACM Transactions on Database Systems*, Vol. 11, No. 2 (June 1986)

Beeri, C., and Kifer, M., "A Comprehensive Approach to the Design of Relational Database Schemes," *Proceedings of the 10th International Conference on Very Large Data Bases*, Singapore (August 1984)

Beeri, C., Mendelson, A. O., Sagiv, Y., and Ullman, J. D., "Equivalence of Relational Database Schemes," *SIAM Journal of Computing*, Vol. 10, No. 2 (May 1981)

Beeri, C., Fagin, R., Maier, D., Mendelson, A. O., Ullman, J. D., and Yannakakis, M., "Properties of Acyclic Database Schemes," *Proceedings of the 13th Annual ACM Symposium on the Theory of Computing*, New York (1981)

Bernstein, P. A., *Normalization and Functional Dependencies in the Relational Data Base Model*, Ph.D. thesis, University of Toronto (1975)

Bernstein, P. A., "Synthesizing Third Normal Form Relations from Functional Dependencies," *ACM Transactions on Database Systems*, Vol. 1, No. 4 (December 1976)

Bernstein, P. A., and Beeri, C., "An Algorithmic Approach to Normalization of Relational Database Schemas," Technical Report CSRG-73, Computer Science Research Group, University of Toronto (1976)

Bernstein, P. A., Swenson, J. R., and Tsichritzis, D. C., "A Unified Approach to Functional Dependencies and Relations," *Proceedings, ACM SIGMOD Conference*, ed. W. F. King, San Jose, Calif. (May 1975)

Biskup, J., Dayal, U., and Bernstein, P. A., "Synthesizing Independent Database Schemes," *Proceedings of the ACM SIGMOD International Conference on Management of Data*, New York (1979)

Cadiou, J. M., "On Semantic Issues in the Relational Model of Data," *Proceedings, International Symposium on Mathematical Foundations of Computer Science*, Gdansk, Poland; also in *Lecture Notes in Computer Science*, Springer-Verlag, Heidelberg (September 1975)

Carlson, C. R., and Kaplan, R. S., "A Generalized Access Path and Its Application to a Relational Data Base System," *Proceedings of the ACM SIGMOD International Conference on Management of Data*, Washington D.C. (June 1976)

Casanova, M. A., Fagin, R., and Papadimitriou, C. M., "Inclusion Dependencies and Their Interaction with Functional Dependencies," *Proceedings, First ACM SIGACT-SIGMOD Symposium on Principles of Database Systems* (March 1982)

Codd, E. F., "Recent Investigations in Relational Data Base Systems," *Information Processing '74*, North-Holland, Amsterdam (1974)

Codd, E. F., "A Relational Model of Data for Large Shared Data Banks," *Communications of the ACM*, Vol. 13, No. 6 (June 1970)

Codd, E. F., "Normalized Data Base Structure: A Brief Tutorial," *Proceedings, 1971 ACM SIGFIDET Workshop on Data Description*, Access and Control (November 1971)

Date, C. J., *An Introduction To Database Systems*, fourth ed., Vol. 1, Addison-Wesley, Reading, Mass. (1985)

Delobel, C., "Normalization and Hierarchical Dependencies in the Relational Data Model," *ACM Transactions on Database Systems,* Vol. 3, No. 3 (1978)

Delobel, C., and Casey, R. G., "Decomposition of a Data Base and the Theory of Boolean Switching Functions," *IBM Journal of Research and Development,* Vol. 17, No. 5 (September 1973)

Delobel, C., and Leonard, M., "The Decomposition Process in a Relational Model," *Proceedings, International Workshop on Data Structure Models for Information Systems,* Pressws University de Namur, Namur, Belgium (May 1974)

Fagin, R., "Acyclic Database Schemes (of Various Degrees): A Painless Introduction," *Proceedings of CAAP* (1983); also in IBM Research Report RJ3800 (April 1983)

Fagin, R., "Horn Clauses and Database Dependencies," IBM Research Report RJ2741 (1980)

Fagin, R., "Functional Dependencies in a Relational Database and Propositional Logic," *IBM Journal of Research and Development,* Vol. 21, No. 6 (November 1977)

Fagin, R., Mendelzon, A. O., and Ullman, J. D., "A Simplified Universal Relation Assumption and Its Properties," *ACM Transactions on Database Systems,* Vol. 7, No. 3 (September 1982)

Fagin, R., and Vardi, M. Y., "The Theory of Data Dependencies—A Survey," IBM Research Report RJ4321 (June 1984)

Furtado, A. L., and Kerschberg, L., "An Algebra of Quotient Relations," *ACM SIGMOD International Conference on Management of Data,* Toronto (1977)

Gyssens, M., "On the Complexity of Join Dependencies," *ACM Transactions on Database Systems,* Vol. 11, No. 1 (March 1986)

Gyssens, M., and Paredaens, J., "A Decomposition Methodology for Cyclic Databases," *Advances in Database Theory,* Vol. 2, Plenum Press, New York (1973)

Gyssens, M., and Paredaens, J., "On the Decomposition of Join Dependencies," *Proceedings of the Third Symposium on Principles of Database Systems,* Waterloo, Ontario (April 1984)

Gyssens, M., "Embedded Join Dependencies as A Tool for Decomposing Full Join Dependencies," *Proceedings of the Fourth Symposium on Principles of Database Systems,* Portland, Ore. (April 1985)

Gyssens, M., "*Decomposition of Join Dependencies in the Relational Database Model,*" Ph.D. thesis, University of Antwerp (June 1985)

Janssens, D., and Paredaens, J., "General Dependencies," Research Report 79-35, University of Antwerp (December 1979)

Kent, W., "A Simple Guide to Five Normal Forms in Relational Database Theory," *Communications of the ACM*, Vol. 26, No. 2 (February 1983)

Kent, W., "Consequences of Assuming a Universal Relation," *ACM Transactions on Database Systems*, Vol. 6, No. 4 (December 1981)

Kent, W., "The Universal Relation Revisited," *ACM Transactions on Database Systems*, Vol. 8, No. 4 (December 1983)

Kifer, M., "Nonconventional Design Theory for Relational Database Schemes," TR 85-07, Department of Computer Science, SUNY at Stony Brook (February 1985)

Lee, T. T., "An Algebraic Theory of Relational Databases," Bell Systems Journal, Vol. 62, No. 10 (December 1983)

Lien, Y. E., "On the Equivalence of Database Models," *Journal of the ACM*, Vol. 29, No. 2 (April 1982)

Lien, Y. E., "Multivalued Dependencies with Null Values in Relational Databases," Fifth International Conference on Very Large Data Bases, Rio De Janeiro (1979)

Maier, D., *The Theory of Relational Databases*, Computer Science Press, Potomac, Md. (1983)

Maier, D., Mendelzon, A. O., and Sagiv, Y., "Testing Implications of Data Dependencies," *Supplement to the ACM SIGMOD International Conference on Management of Data*, Boston (1979); also in *ACM Transactions on Database Systems*, Vol. 4, No. 4 (1980)

Maier, D., and Ullman, J., "Fragments of Relations," Proceedings, 1983 ACM SIGMOD International Conference on Management of Data (May 1983)

Maier, D., and Ullman, J., "Maximal Objects and the Semantics of Universal Relational Databases," *ACM Transactions of Database Systems*, Vol. 8, No. 1 (March 1983)

Maier, D., Ullman, J. D., and Yardi, M. S., "On the Foundations of the Universal Relation Model," *ACM Transactions on Database Systems*, Vol. 9, No. 2 (June 1984)

Maier, D., Ullman, J. D., and Yardi, M. S., "The Revenge of the JD," Proceedings, *Second ACM SIGACT-SIGMOD Symposium on Principles of Database Systems* (March 1983)

Mendelson, A. O., and Maier, D., "Generalized Mutual Dependencies and the Decomposition of Database Relations," Fifth International Conference on Very Large Data Bases, Rio de Janeiro (1979)

Nicolas, J. M., "Mutual Dependencies and Some Results on Undecomposable Relations," Fourth International Conference on Very Large Data Bases, Berlin (1978)

Parker, D. S., and Delobel, C., "Algorithmic Applications for a New Result on Multivalued Dependencies," *Proceedings, Fifth International Conference on Very Large Data Bases*, Rio de Janeiro (October 1979)

Paredaens, J., and Gallaire, H., "Transitive Dependencies in Data Base Schemas", *R.A.I.R.O. Informatique/Computer Science*, Vol. 14, No. 2 (1980)

Paredaens, J., and Van Gucht, D., "An Application of the Theory of Graphs and Hypergraphs to the Decompositions of Relational Database Schemes," *Proceedings of CAAP* (1983)

Rissanen, J., "Theory of Joins For Relational Databases—A Tutorial Survey," *Proceedings of the Seventh Symposium on the Mathematical Foundations of Computer Science*, Lecture Notes in Computer Science 64, Springer Verlag (1978)

Rissanen, J., "Independent Components of Relations," Research Report RJ1899, IBM Research Laboratory, San Jose, Calif. (January 1977); also in *ACM Transactions on Database Systems*, Vol. 2, No. 4 (December 1977)

Sadi, F., and Ullman, J. D., "A Complete Axiomatization for a Large Class of Dependencies in Relational Databases," *Proceedings, 12th Annual ACM Symposium on Theory of Computing* (1980)

Sagiv, Y., "A Characterization of Globally Consistent Databases and Their Correct Access Paths," *ACM Transactions on Database Systems*, Vol. 8, No. 2 (June 1983)

Sagiv, Y., and Fagin, R., "An Equivalence between Relational Database Dependencies and a Subclass of Propositional Logic," IBM Research Report RJ2500 (March 1979)

Sagiv, Y., Delobel, C., Parker, D. S., and Fagin, R., "An Equivalence between Relational Database Dependencies and a Subclass of Propositional Logic," *Journal of the ACM*, Vol. 28, No. 3 (June 1981)

Sagiv, Y., and Walecka, S., "Subset Dependencies as an Alternative to Embedded Multivalued Dependencies," UIUCDS-R-79-980, UILU-ENG 79 1732, Department of Computer Science, University of Illinois at Urbana-Champaign (July 1979)

Schmid, M. A., and Swenson, J. R., "On the Semantics of the Relational Data Model," *Proceedings, ACM SIGMOD International Conference on Management of Data*, San Jose, Calif. (May 1975)

Sciore, E., "Real-world MVDs," Technical Report 80/014, Department of Computer Science, SUNY at Stony Brook (November 1980)

Sciore, E., "Improving Database Schemes by Adding Attributes," ACM PODS (1983)

Sciore, E., *The Universal Instance and Database Design*, TR 271, Ph.D. thesis, Princeton University (June 1980)

Smith, J. M., "A Normal Form for Abstract Syntax," *Proceedings of the Fourth International Conference on Very Large Database Systems*, West Berlin (September 1978)

Ullman, J. D., *Principles of Database Systems*, Computer Science Press, Potomac, Md. (1980)

Ullman, J. D., *Principles of Database Systems*, Second ed., Pitman, Marshfield, Mass. (1982)

Ullman, J. D., "The Universal Relation Strikes Back," *Proceedings, First ACM SIGACT-SIGMOD Symposium on Principles of Database Systems* (March 1982)

Yannakakis, M., and Papadimitiriou, C. M., "Algebraic Dependencies," M.I.T. Research Report (1980)

Zaniolo, C., *Analysis and Design of Relational Schemata for Database Systems*, Ph.D. thesis, Technical Report UCLA-ENG-7669, University of California, Los Angeles (July 1976)

Zaniolo, C., and Melkanoff, M. A., "On the Design of Relational Database Schemata," *ACM Transactions on Database Systems*, Vol. 6, No. 1 (March 1981)

# Solutions to Odd Numbered Exercises

**Chapter 2**

2.1  a. Yes, although the missing data will create problems. Null values in the primary key violate the relational model.

     b. No, rows 2 and 5 are duplicates.

     c. No, attributes A and C both contain data of more than one type.

2.3  a. Yes, the student's number will define an advisor. Thus:

$$ADVISOR = f\ (NUM)$$
$$NUM \rightarrow ADVISOR$$

     b. No, ADVISOR could define many values of NUM (assuming an advisor can have more than one student). Thus:

$$NUM \neq f\ (ADVISOR)$$
$$ADVISOR \nrightarrow NUM$$

2.5  a. NUM is the best choice. NAME might be used, but two students could have the same name. ADVISOR cannot be a candidate key since ADVISOR could define more than one student.

     b. No, because NAME could be removed without invalidating the unique identification.

2.7  $AB \rightarrow C$ and $AC \rightarrow B$

2.9  a. True (axiom 3)

     b. False

     c. True (axiom 2)

     d. False

     e. True (axiom 2)

2.11 a. True (axiom 5)
 b. True (axioms 5 and 3)
 c. True (axiom 2)
 d. True (axiom 2)
 e. True (axioms 5, 3 and 2)

2.13 R1(<u>INUM</u>, IDATE)
 R2(<u>INUM, CNUM</u>, ITEMN, QUANT, PRICE)

2.15

| a. A | b. B | c. C | d. A B | e. B C |
|------|------|------|--------|--------|
| 1    | 1    | 1    | 1 1    | 1 1    |
|      | 2    | 2    | 1 2    | 2 2    |
|      | 3    | 3    | 1 3    | 3 3    |
|      |      |      |        | 1 2    |
|      |      |      |        | 2 1    |

2.17 a. Union: {A, B, C, D, E, F, G}
 Intersection: {A}
 R1 – R2: {B, C, D} R2 – R1: {E, F, G}
 b. Union: {A, B, C, D}
 Intersection: {A, B, C, D}
 R1 – R2: empty set R2 – R1: empty set
 c. Union: {A, B, C, D}
 Intersection: {A, B}
 R1 – R2: {C, D} R2 – R1: empty set
 d. Union: {A, B, C, D, E, F}
 Intersection: empty set
 R1 – R2: {A, B, C} R2 – R1: {D, E, F}
 e. Union: {A, B, C, D}
 Intersection: {A, C}
 R1 – R2: {D} R2 – R1: {B}

## Chapter 3

3.1 Multiple sections of the same class are not allowed unless the class name somehow reflects the multiple possible sections.

3.3 a. Third normal form since PNUM → INVENTORY and PNUM → RESERVE and no transitive dependencies exist.
 b. Second normal form. The relation is not in third normal form since INVENTORY, RESERVE → AVAILABLE FOR SALE.

Note that AVAILABLE FOR SALE is a linear combination of INVENTORY and RESERVE. Attributes that can be directly calculated from other attributes need not exist physically in the database. The trade-off between physical space and calculation time must be considered.

3.5   No, the transitive dependency will still exist. For example, dependencies $A \rightarrow B$, $A \rightarrow C$ and $B \rightarrow C$ will be satisfied with the following data although duplicates in the B attribute occur:

| A | B | C |
|---|---|---|
| 1 | 1 | 2 |
| 5 | 2 | 3 |
| 2 | 1 | 2 |

$B \longrightarrow A$ is one dependency that will allow a single relation to be created. Adding $B \longrightarrow A$ will make B a superkey, and thus the relation would now be in third normal form. This dependency will require a change in the preceding data, such as:

| A | B | C |
|---|---|---|
| 2 | 1 | 2 |
| 5 | 2 | 3 |
| 2 | 1 | 2 |

This change results in a duplicate row. After the duplicate row is removed, B no longer contains duplicate values and the transitive dependency is eliminated.

3.7   a. Yes. Since $A \rightarrow B$ and $B \rightarrow C$, then $A \rightarrow C$. Thus attribute A implies both of the other attributes in the relation and A is a candidate key.

   b. No. Attribute B is not a candidate key since dependencies $A \rightarrow B$ and $B \rightarrow C$ do not imply that $B \rightarrow A$. Thus $B \nrightarrow A$, and thus B cannot be a candidate key.

   c. No. Attribute C is not a candidate key because the dependencies do not imply that $C \rightarrow A$ or $C \rightarrow B$. Thus $C \nrightarrow A$ and C cannot be a candidate key. Also, $C \nrightarrow B$ is sufficient to disqualify C as a candidate key.

3.9   Yes, since B is a member of the key.

3.11  No, since BC is not a superkey and D does not belong to a key.

3.13  Yes, since B is a superkey (B is also a candidate key).

## Chapter 4

4.1 a. Yes. The instance is valid since:
- No duplicate rows exist in attribute A.
- The rows containing duplicate values in B also contain duplicate values in C.

b. No. The relation is not in third normal form since $B \rightarrow C$ and C is not part of the primary key.

c. No. The relation is not in Boyce-Codd normal form since $B \rightarrow C$ and B is not a superkey.

4.3 a. Yes. The only dependency is $AB \rightarrow C$.

b.

| A | B | C |
|---|---|---|
| 1 | 1 | 1 |
| 1 | 2 | 1 |

c. No. C is not a superkey, as the instance in part b shows.

4.5 a. False
b. True (axiom 1)
c. True (axiom 2)
d. False
e. False

4.7 a. True (axiom 4)
b. True (axiom 4)
c. True (axiom 4)
d. True (axioms 3 and 7)
e. True (axiom 3)

4.9 a. True (axiom 6)
b. False
c. False
d. (Also holds for part e.) True, since any multivalued dependency is trivially true if the dependency uses all of the defined attributes.
e. See part d.

4.11 a. False
b. False
c. True (axiom 3 or since the dependency uses all the attributes)
d. True (axiom 8)
e. True (axiom 7)

4.13 a.

| A | B | C | D |
|---|---|---|---|
| 1 | 5 | 9 | 1 |
| 2 | 6 | 10 | 1 |
| 3 | 7 | 11 | 1 |
| 3 | 7 | 12 | 1 |

b.

| A | B | C | D |
|---|---|---|---|
| 1 | 5 | 9 | 1 |
| 2 | 6 | 10 | 1 |
| 3 | 7 | 11 | 1 |
| 3 | 7 | 12 | 2 |

c.

| A | B | C | D |
|---|---|---|---|
| 1 | 5 | 9 | 1 |
| 2 | 6 | 10 | 1 |
| 2 | 7 | 11 | 1 |
| 2 | 7 | 12 | 1 |

d.

| A | B | C | D |
|---|---|---|---|
| 1 | 5 | 9 | 1 |
| 2 | 6 | 10 | 1 |
| 2 | 7 | 11 | 1 |
| 2 | 7 | 12 | 2 |

4.15 a.

| A | B | C | D |
|---|---|---|---|
| 1 | 2 | 6 | 10 |
| 1 | 2 | 6 | 9 |
| 3 | 4 | 7 | 3 |
| 5 | 6 | 8 | 6 |

b.

| A | B | C | D |
|---|---|---|---|
| 1 | 2 | 6 | 10 |
| 2 | 2 | 6 | 9 |
| 3 | 4 | 7 | 3 |
| 5 | 6 | 8 | 6 |

c.

| A | B | C | D |
|---|---|---|---|
| 1 | 2 | 6 | 10 |
| 1 | 3 | 6 | 9 |
| 3 | 4 | 7 | 3 |
| 3 | 4 | 7 | 6 |

d.

| A | B | C | D |
|---|---|---|---|
| 1 | 2 | 6 | 10 |
| 1 | 3 | 6 | 9 |
| 3 | 4 | 7 | 3 |
| 5 | 4 | 7 | 6 |

e.

| A | B | C | D |
|---|---|---|---|
| 1 | 2 | 6 | 10 |
| 1 | 2 | 10 | 9 |
| 3 | 4 | 7 | 3 |
| 5 | 6 | 8 | 6 |

## Chapter 5

**5.1** An obvious choice is:

R1(<u>EMPLOYEE</u>, DEPARTMENT, JOB TITLE)
R2(<u>JOB TITLE</u>, JOB LEVEL)

Two other choices are:

R1(<u>EMPLOYEE</u>, JOB TITLE)
R2(<u>EMPLOYEE</u>, DEPARTMENT, JOB LEVEL)

R1(<u>EMPLOYEE</u>, JOB LEVEL)
R2(<u>EMPLOYEE</u>, DEPARTMENT, JOB TITLE)

**5.3**  **a.** Yes. The new relation contains seven rows although the original relation contained only five rows. The two new invalid rows are indicated with a ** notation:

| A | B | C | D |   |
|---|---|---|---|---|
| 1 | 1 | 1 | 1 |   |
| 1 | 1 | 1 | 2 | ** |
| 2 | 1 | 2 | 1 | ** |
| 2 | 1 | 2 | 2 |   |
| 2 | 2 | 3 | 3 |   |
| 3 | 2 | 3 | 3 |   |
| 3 | 3 | 3 | 4 |   |

**b.** Yes. The new relation contains nine rows although the original relation contained only five rows. The four new invalid rows are indicated with a ** notation:

| A | B | C | D |   |
|---|---|---|---|---|
| 1 | 1 | 1 | 1 |   |
| 2 | 1 | 2 | 2 |   |
| 2 | 1 | 2 | 3 | ** |
| 2 | 2 | 3 | 2 | ** |
| 2 | 2 | 3 | 3 |   |
| 3 | 2 | 3 | 3 |   |
| 3 | 2 | 3 | 4 | ** |
| 3 | 3 | 3 | 3 | ** |
| 3 | 3 | 3 | 4 |   |

**c.** This sequence of joins will recreate the original database with no extraneous information. The details follow:

| Relation 2 |   |   | Relation 3 |   |   | Relation 2 x 3 |   |   |
|---|---|---|---|---|---|---|---|---|
| **B** | **D** |   | **A** | **D** |   | **A** | **B** | **D** |
| 1 | 1 |   | 1 | 1 |   | 1 | 1 | 1 |
| 1 | 2 | x | 2 | 2 | = | 2 | 1 | 2 |
| 2 | 3 |   | 2 | 3 |   | 2 | 2 | 3 |
| 3 | 4 |   | 3 | 3 |   | 3 | 2 | 3 |
|   |   |   | 3 | 4 |   | 3 | 3 | 4 |

| Relation 1 | | | | Relation 2 x 3 | | | | Relation 1 x (Relation 2 x 3) | | | |
|---|---|---|---|---|---|---|---|---|---|---|---|
| **A** | **B** | **C** | | **A** | **B** | **D** | | **A** | **B** | **C** | **D** |
| 1 | 1 | 1 | | 1 | 1 | 1 | | 1 | 1 | 1 | 1 |
| 2 | 1 | 2 | x | 2 | 1 | 2 | = | 2 | 1 | 2 | 2 |
| 2 | 2 | 3 | | 2 | 2 | 3 | | 2 | 2 | 3 | 3 |
| 3 | 2 | 3 | | 3 | 2 | 3 | | 3 | 2 | 3 | 3 |
| 3 | 3 | 3 | | 3 | 3 | 4 | | 3 | 3 | 3 | 4 |

5.5   a. R1($\underline{A}$, $\underline{C}$, D)
      R2($\underline{A}$, B)
   b. R1($\underline{A}$, $\underline{C}$)
      R2($\underline{A}$, B)
      R3($\underline{B}$, $\underline{C}$, D)

5.7   a. (Also holds for part b.) Since R1 and R2 do not satisfy the lossless join property, then neither multivalued dependency can be true. Alternatively, note that an invalid row ( 1 2 1 ) is created by interchanging C in rows 3 and 4. Thus B ⇸ C. Then B ⇸ A must also be true. Or note that an invalid row ( 2 2 2 ) is created by interchanging A in rows 3 and 4. Thus B ⇸ A and therefore B ⇸ C is also true.
   b. See part a.

c.

| A | B |
|---|---|
| 1 | 1 |
| 1 | 2 |
| 2 | 2 |
| 2 | 1 |

d.

| B | C |
|---|---|
| 1 | 1 |
| 2 | 2 |
| 2 | 1 |
| 1 | 2 |

e.

| A | B | C | |
|---|---|---|---|
| 1 | 1 | 1 | |
| 1 | 1 | 2 | |
| 1 | 2 | 2 | |
| 1 | 2 | 1 | ** |
| 2 | 2 | 2 | ** |
| 2 | 2 | 1 | |
| 2 | 1 | 1 | |
| 2 | 1 | 2 | |

   f. No. The rows indicated with ** are invalid.

5.9   The following sequences satisfy the conditions of the problem:

|  |  |  |  |  |
|---|---|---|---|---|
| R1 | x | R2 | x | R3 |
| R2 | x | R3 | x | R1 |
| R2 | x | R1 | x | R3 |
| R3 | x | R2 | x | R1 |

For example, consider the sequence R1 x R2 x R3. The join R1 x R2 is lossless if either A → B or A → CD. Since A → B, the join is lossless.

Then (R1 x R2) x R3 is lossless if either D → E or D → ABC. Since D → E, the entire join sequence is lossless.

5.11 The following sequences satisfy the conditions of the problem:

| | | | | | | | |
|---|---|---|---|---|---|---|---|
| R3 | x | R4 | x | R2 | x | R1 |
| R3 | x | R4 | x | R1 | x | R2 |
| R2 | x | R4 | x | R3 | x | R1 |
| R4 | x | R3 | x | R2 | x | R1 |
| R4 | x | R3 | x | R1 | x | R2 |
| R4 | x | R2 | x | R3 | x | R1 |

For example, consider the sequence R1 x R2 x R3 x R4. The join R1 x R2 is lossless if either D → AC or D → B. Since D → B, the join is lossless. Then (R1 x R2) x R3 is lossless if either A → E or A → BCD. Neither of these dependencies is true, and thus the join sequence is not lossless. The implied dependency AD → C must be used to correctly identify all the sequences that satisfy the lossless join.

5.13 The following sequences satisfy the conditions of the problem:

$$(R1 \times R2) \times (R3 \times R4)$$
$$(R2 \times R1) \times (R3 \times R4)$$
$$(R1 \times R2) \times (R4 \times R3)$$
$$(R2 \times R1) \times (R4 \times R3)$$
$$(R3 \times R4) \times (R1 \times R2)$$
$$(R3 \times R4) \times (R2 \times R1)$$
$$(R4 \times R3) \times (R1 \times R2)$$
$$(R4 \times R3) \times (R2 \times R1)$$

Note that ((R1 x R2) x R3) x R4 is not lossless.

5.15 a. A → D
b. BC → A
c. A → D and BC → A

5.17 a. A ↠ B/C and B → E
b. CD ↠ B/A
c. A ↠ B/C, CD ↠ B/A and B → E

5.19 a. (R1 x R2) x R3 or R1 x (R2 x R3)
b. None. All the attributes can be joined losslessly.
c. None. All the relations can be joined losslessly.
d. None.

5.21 a. (R4 x R8) x R6 or R4 x (R8 x R6)
b. HPUR cannot be joined losslessly with CPER, CEXT, CLOC, SNAME, STYPE, SVER, SRATE or SPUR.

c. R1 cannot be joined losslessly with R4, R6, R8 or R9.
d. Add SNAME and SVER as key attributes in R1.

## Chapter 6

**6.1**  Eliminate MTITLE → CLASS

**6.3**  a. (R7 x R3) x R2
b. R1 x R2
c. ((R7 x R8) x R5) x R3
d. (R8 x R6) x R1
e. R1 x R2
f. ((R5 x R8) x R4) x R2
g. ((R7 x R8) x R3) x R1
h. ((R7 x R8) x R3) x R5

## Chapter 7

**7.1**  SELECT   FNAME, MNAME, LNAME, PAY
FROM     R5, R8
WHERE    R5.SSNUM = R8.SSNUM
         AND
         PNUM < 100

The result is the following instance:

| FNAME | MNAME | LNAME | PAY |
|-------|-------|-------|-----|
| Kara | Michelle | Divinski | 54000 |
| Mark | Richard | Chibit | 38000 |
| Sarah | Stacy | Thomas | 25000 |
| Amy | Barbara | Smith | 31000 |
| Thomas | Charles | Easterwood | 38000 |
| Kim | Erin | Jones | 31000 |
| Adam | Josh | Smith | 24000 |
| Lauren | Angela | Easterwood | 20000 |
| Betsy | Kate | Blair | 89000 |
| Vanessa | Martha | Smith | 18000 |
| Karen | Cheryl | Brown | 18000 |

7.3   SELECT   FNAME, MNAME, LNAME, CDATE
      FROM     R5, R8
      WHERE    CCODE = "Nh"
               AND
               CDATE < Dec 31 1981
               AND
               R5.SSNUM = R8.SSNUM

The result is the following instance:

| FNAME | MNAME | LNAME | CDATE |
|-------|-------|-------|-------|
| Kara | Michelle | Divinski | Jun 23 1974 |
| Amy | Barbara | Smith | Sep 1 1980 |
| Betsy | Kate | Blair | Mar 1 1976 |

7.5   SELECT   FNAME, MNAME, LNAME
      FROM     R2, R8, R5
      WHERE    PSUP = 003
               AND
               R2.PNUM = R8.PNUM
               AND
               R8.SSNUM = R5.SSNUM

The result is the following instance:

| FNAME | MNAME | LNAME |
|-------|-------|-------|
| Lauren | Angela | Easterwood |
| Amy | Barbara | Smith |
| Kim | Erin | Jones |

**7.7**  SELECT   DFNAME, DLNAME, DBDATE
     FROM    R1, R2, R8, R6, R7
     WHERE   DEPTNAME = "Controller"
             AND
             R1.DEPTNUM = R2.DEPTNUM
             AND
             R2.PNUM = R8.PNUM
             AND
             R8.SSNUM = R6.SSNUM
             AND
             HR = "W"
             AND
             R6.DSSNUM = R7.DSSNUM

The result is the following instance:

| DFNAME | DLNAME | DBDATE |
|--------|--------|--------|
| Amy | Smith | Mar 8 1939 |

**7.9**  SELECT   DFNAME, DLNAME
     FROM    R11, R6, R7
     WHERE   SCHOOL = "University of Fairport"
             AND
             R11.SSNUM = R6.SSNUM
             AND
             HR = "C"
             AND
             R6.DSSNUM = R7.DSSNUM

No such children exist. The only graduates of the University of Fairport are Thomas and Lauren Easterwood, who have no children.

7.11  SELECT  FNAME, MNAME, LNAME, BDATE, CDATE
      FROM    R5, R8
      WHERE   R5.SSNUM = R8.SSNUM
              AND
              BDATE < Jan 1 1945
              AND
              CCODE = "Nh"
              AND
              CDATE < Jan 1 1983

The result is the following instance:

| FNAME | MNAME | LNAME | BDATE | CDATE |
|-------|-------|-------|-------|-------|
| Amy | Barbara | Smith | Mar 8 1939 | Sep 1 1980 |
| Betsy | Kate | Blair | Jan 6 1941 | Mar 1 1976 |

7.13  SELECT  FNAME, MNAME, LNAME, PTITLE
      FROM    R8, R5, R2
      WHERE   R8.SSNUM = R5.SSNUM
              AND
              R8.PNUM = R2.PNUM
              AND
              CCODE = "Pr"
              AND
              CDATE < Jan 1 1986
              AND
              CDATE > Dec 31 1984

The result is the following instance:

| FNAME | MNAME | LNAME | PTITLE |
|-------|-------|-------|--------|
| Mark | Richard | Chibit | Manager, purchasing |

**7.15** The join is lossless since SSNUM is the intersection of R5 and R8 and SSNUM is the key of R5.

**7.17** R1 x R2 is lossless since DEPT is the intersection of R1 and R2 and DEPT is the key of R1.

(R1 x R2) x R8 is lossless since PNUM is the intersection of (R1 x R2) and R8 and PNUM is the key of R1 x R2.

(R1 x R2 x R8) x R6 is the potential problem. However, SSNUM $\twoheadrightarrow$ DSSNUM, HR in the context of the other attributes in R1 x R2 x R8.

(R1 x R2 x R8 x R6) x R7 is lossless since DSSNUM is the intersection of R1 x R2 x R8 x R6 and R7 and DSSNUM is the key for R7.

## Chapter 8

**8.1** SSNUM and DATESCH, NAME and DATESCH, CNUM and DNUM, CNUM and DNAME, CNUM and BEGDATE, CDESC and DNUM, CDESC and DNAME, CDESC and BEGDATE, CREDITS and DNUM, CREDITS and DNAME, CREDITS and BEGDATE, DNUM and SDATE, DNUM and GRADE, DNUM and DATESCH, DNAME and SDATE, DNAME and GRADE, DNAME and DATESCH, SDATE and DATESCH, SDATE and BEGDATE, GRADE and DATESCH, GRADE and BEGDATE, DATESCH and BEGDATE

8.3   a.

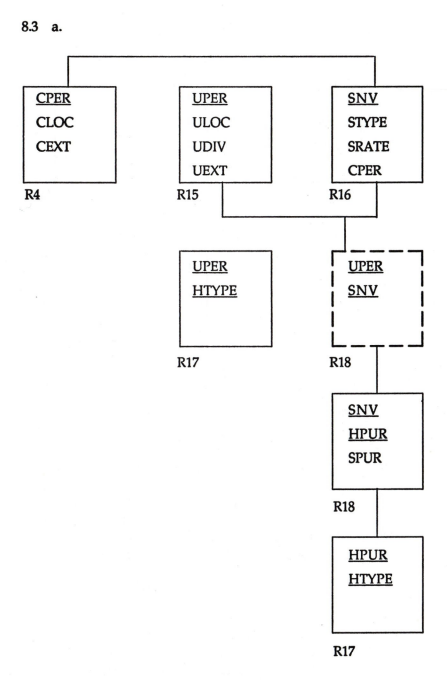

More efficient designs can be generated, depending upon the software in use.

b.

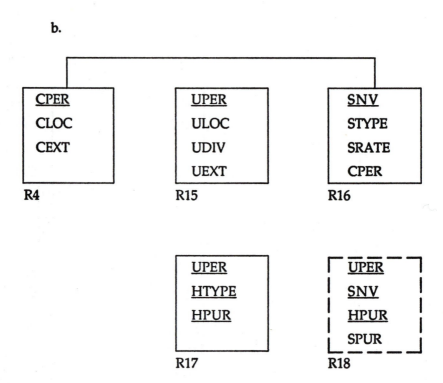

| CPER | UPER | SNV |
|------|------|-----|
| CLOC | ULOC | STYPE |
| CEXT | UDIV | SRATE |
|      | UEXT | CPER |

R4              R15              R16

| UPER | UPER |
|------|------|
| HTYPE | SNV |
| HPUR | HPUR |
|      | SPUR |

R17              R18

## Chapter 9

**9.1**  a. Yes. The relation is in third normal form since the only dependencies are A → B and A → C.

b. Yes. The relation is in Boyce-Codd normal form since the only dependencies are A → B and A → C and A is a superkey.

**9.3**  a. No. The relation is not in third normal form since A → B and B is not part of the primary key and A is not a superkey.

b. Yes. AC → B since AC is the primary key.

**9.5**  a. Yes. AB is a superkey since A is a candidate key. Therefore the relation is in third normal form.

b. Yes. The relation is in Boyce-Codd normal form since AB is a superkey.

c. Yes. AB ↠ C since AB → C.

d. Yes. Note that the intersection of ABC and ABD is AB, which can contain no duplicate rows in a valid instance.

**9.7**  a. No. The relational schema is not in projection-join normal form. The fact that BC is the key does not imply that the lossless join constraint holds.

    **b.** No. The fact that BC is the key does not imply that $B \rightarrow C$. Also, R1(A, B) x R2(B, C) can be lossless without $B \rightarrow C$.

    **c.** No. Nothing in the relational schema requires AD to be a superkey. Therefore AD cannot be a candidate key.

**9.9**   **a.** Yes. $B \twoheadrightarrow C$ since R1(A, B) x R2(B, C) is lossless.

    **b.** No. Nothing in the relational schema requires that B is a superkey.

    **c.** No. The fact that A is the key does not imply that R1(A, B) x R2(B, C) is lossless.

    **d.** No. Since R1(A, B) x R2(B, C) is lossless, then $B \twoheadrightarrow A$ and $B \twoheadrightarrow C$. However, B is not a superkey. Therefore the relation is not in fourth normal form.

## Chapter 10

**10.1**   **a.** No, since neither $A \twoheadrightarrow C$ nor $A \twoheadrightarrow B$ is established.

    **b.** No, since neither $B \twoheadrightarrow C$ nor $B \twoheadrightarrow A$ is established.

    **c.** No, since neither $C \twoheadrightarrow A$ nor $C \twoheadrightarrow B$ is established.

    **d.** Yes, since $A \leftrightarrow B$.

    **e.** Yes, since the lossless join property was established in part d.

    **f.** Yes, since the lossless join property was established in part d.

**10.3**   **a.** ( 1 1 2 )

    **b.** None

    **c.** ( 1 1 2 ), ( 1 2 1 ), ( 2 1 1 ) and ( 2 2 2 )

    **d.** None

**10.5**   **a.** Yes. Since $A \twoheadrightarrow B$, the join of projections R(A, B) and R(A, C) is lossless. Therefore $A \leftrightarrow B$.

    **b.** No. Constraint $A \twoheadrightarrow B$ does not require that $A \rightarrow B$.

    **c.** Yes. $A \twoheadrightarrow C$ because $A \twoheadrightarrow B$ and A, B and C are the only attributes in the relation.

**10.7**

| A | B | C | |
|---|---|---|---|
| 1 | 1 | 1 | |
| 2 | 1 | 1 | ** |
| 1 | 2 | 2 | |
| 2 | 2 | 2 | ** |
| 1 | 1 | 2 | ** |
| 2 | 1 | 2 | |
| 1 | 2 | 1 | ** |
| 2 | 2 | 1 | |

$A \leftrightarrow B$ is not satisfied since four invalid rows are created.

10.9   a. No, since AB x AC x AD is not lossless.
       b. Yes, since CDA x AB is lossless.
       c. No, since AB x BC x BD does not satisfy the lossless join property.
       d. Yes, since AB x ACD is lossless.

10.11  a. If A $\twoheadrightarrow$ B, then AB x AC is lossless; thus A: B\C. If A: B\C, then
          AB x AC is lossless; therefore A $\twoheadrightarrow$ B.
       b. No. A $\rightarrow$ B is a sufficient but not a necessary condition for AB
          x AC to have a lossless join. Thus A $\rightarrow$ B implies A: B\C, but
          A: B\C does not imply A $\rightarrow$ B.
       c. Yes. Since A: B\C, then AB x AC is lossless. Therefore (AB x AC)
          x BC is lossless since joining ABC with a subset of ABC cannot
          create any rows that are not in an instance of ABC. Thus A $\leftrightarrow$ B.
       d. No. If AB x AC x BC is a lossless join, this does not imply that AB
          x AC is also lossless. Joining BC with AB x AC can eliminate
          fictitious rows in an instance of ABC, thus making (AB x AC) x
          BC lossless.

10.13  $2^7 - 2$

       The join AB x AC x AD x AE x AF x AG x AH must be lossless. The
       join AB x AC yields four rows ($2^2$). The join (AB x AC) x AD yields
       eight rows ($2^3$). The join {(AB x AC) x AD} x AE yields sixteen rows
       ($2^4$). The six joins will thus yield $2^7$ rows.

10.15  a. None. The join AB x AC x AD gives the following instance:

| A | B | C | D |
|---|---|---|---|
| 1 | 1 | 1 | 1 |
| 1 | 1 | 1 | 2 |
| 1 | 1 | 2 | 1 |
| 1 | 2 | 1 | 1 |
| 1 | 2 | 2 | 2 |
| 1 | 2 | 2 | 1 |
| 1 | 2 | 1 | 2 |
| 1 | 1 | 2 | 2 |

Joining this to the projection on BC removes some rows to give
the following instance:

| A | B | C | D |
|---|---|---|---|
| 1 | 1 | 1 | 1 |
| 1 | 1 | 1 | 2 |
| 1 | 2 | 2 | 2 |
| 1 | 2 | 2 | 1 |

Joining this to the projection on CD removes more rows to give the following instance:

| A | B | C | D |
|---|---|---|---|
| 1 | 1 | 1 | 1 |
| 1 | 2 | 2 | 2 |

The join AB x AC x AD x BC x CD is thus lossless, and no rows need be added to make the instance valid.

b. ( 1 1 1 2 ), ( 1 2 1 1 )

c. None. The A values in the two rows are different, and thus AB x AC x AD is lossless.

10.17  A: B\C\D means that AB x AC x AD is lossless. A == B\C\D means that AB x AC x AD x BC x CD is lossless. These are not equivalent. Dependency A: B\C\D implies A == B\C\D. However, A == B\C\D does not imply A: B\C\D.

## Appendix

A.1   a. True. Since $G(AB) \leq G(C)$, pairs of rows in $AB$ that map to 1 will also map to 1 in $C$ in all valid instances. Therefore, $AB \rightarrow C$.

b. False. $G(AB) \leq G(C)$ does not imply that $G(AB) \leq G(D)$.

c. True. $AB \twoheadrightarrow C$ since $G(AB) \leq G(C)$; that is, $AB \rightarrow C$.

d. True. $AB \twoheadrightarrow D$ since $AB \twoheadrightarrow C$ and $D$ is the only other attribute in the relation.

e. False. $G(AB) \leq G(C)$ does not imply that $G(C) \leq G(A)$.

A.3   a. True. $G(X) \leq G(Y)$ since if $g_{i,j}(X) = 1$, then $g_{i,j}(Y) = 1$ since $Y$ is contained in $X$.

b. False. It is possible for $g_{i,j}(Y) = 1$ and $g_{i,j}(X) = 0$ if rows $i, j$ contain duplicate values in $A$ but do not contain duplicate values in $BC$.

c. True. Suppose that $g_{i,j}(X) = 1$ and that $g_{i,j}(Z) = 1$. Then rows $i, j$ would be duplicate in $R(A, B, C, D)$ since $XZ = ABCD$. A relation cannot contain duplicate rows in either $g_{i,j}(X) = 0$ or $g_{i,j}(Z) = 0$.

d. False. It is possible for rows $i, j$ to exist such that $g_{i,j}(X) = 1$ and $g_{i,j}(Y) = 1$. In fact, if $g_{i,j}(X) = 1$, then also $g_{i,j}(Y) = 1$ since $Y$ is contained in $X$.

e. True. $X \cap Z$ is contained in $X$. $X \cap Z$ is the attribute $C$. Therefore, if $g_{i,j}(X) = 1$, then $g_{i,j}(C) = 1$ since the rows $i, j$ must be identical in all three of the attributes $A$, $B$ and $C$, which comprise $X$.

f. False. $X \cap Z$ is the attribute $C$. It is possible that a pair of rows contain identical values in $C$ but not in $A$ or $B$. Thus a pair of rows $i, j$ can exist such that $g_{i,j}(C) = 1$ and $g_{i,j}(X) = 0$. Thus the inequality $G(X \cap Z) \leq G(X)$ is false.

g. True. If $g_{i,j}(Z) = 0$, then $g_{i,j}(Z) \cdot g_{i,j}(Z) = 0$. Also, if $g_{i,j}(Z) = 1$, then $g_{i,j}(Z) \cdot g_{i,j}(Z) = 1$.

A.5   $G(X) \leq G(Y)$ and $G(Y) \leq G(Z)$ in all valid $r$. Therefore $G(X) \leq G(Z)$ and thus $X \rightarrow Z$.

A.7   Let $r$ be any valid instance of $R$. If $G(X) = 0$, then $X \rightarrow YZ$. If $g_{i,j}(X) = 1$ for some pair $(i, j)$ in $r$, then $g_{i,j}(Y) = 1$ and $g_{i,j}(Z) = 1$ since $X \rightarrow Y$ and $Y \rightarrow Z$. Therefore $g_{i,j}(YZ) = 1$ and thus $G(X) \leq G(YZ)$.

A.9   The relation is in third normal form if $G(B) = 0$. Suppose that there is an instance in which $g_{i,j}(B) = 1$ for some pair $(i,j)$. Then $g_{i,j}(A) = 1$ and $g_{i,j}(C) = 1$ since $G(B) \leq G(A)$ and $G(B) \leq G(C)$. But then $g_{i,j}(R) = 1$ which is a contradiction since $G(R) = 0$. Therefore $G(B) = 0$.

A.11  The set for $A \rightarrow B$ is $R$. The set for $A \rightarrow C$ is $R$. The set for $B \rightarrow C$ is $\{B,C\}$. Therefore the relation is not in Boyce-Codd normal form.

A.13  Rows $k_1$ and $k_2$ such that:

$$g_{i,k_1}(B) = 1 \quad \text{and} \quad g_{j,k_1}(AC) = 1$$
$$g_{j,k_2}(B) = 1 \quad \text{and} \quad g_{i,k_2}(AC) = 1$$

A.15  Let $r$ be a valid instance. If $g_{i,j}(A) = 0$ for all $(i,j)$ in $r$, then $A \twoheadrightarrow C$ since $G(A) = 0$. If $g_{i,j}(A) = 1$, then there are rows $k_1$ and $k_2$ in $r$ such that:

$$g_{i,k_1}(B) = 1 \qquad\qquad g_{j,k_1}(AC) = 1$$

and

$$g_{j,k_2}(B) = 1 \qquad\qquad g_{i,k_2}(AC) = 1$$

Since

$$g_{j,k_1}(AC) = 1 \qquad g_{j,k_1}(A) = g_{j,k_1}(C) = 1$$
$$g_{i,k_2}(AC) = 1 \qquad g_{i,k_2}(A) = g_{i,k_2}(C) = 1$$

Then, since $g_{i,j}(A) = 1, g_{i,k1}(A) = 1, g_{j,k2}(A) = 1$:

$$g_{i,k1}(AB) = 1, g_{j,k1}(C) = 1, g_{j,k2}(AB) = 1,$$
$$g_{i,k2}(C) = 1$$

Therefore $A \twoheadrightarrow C$.

A.17  $AB \twoheadrightarrow C$ is the only multivalued dependency and it is trivial.

A.19  $C \twoheadrightarrow AD$ and $C \twoheadrightarrow B$.

# Index

(Boldface indicates that a definition is provided on that page.)